Uphill Both Ways Barefooted

A MEMOIR

'THE' HILL

David H. Halsey

HERITAGE BOOKS
2008

HERITAGE BOOKS
AN IMPRINT OF HERITAGE BOOKS, INC.

Books, CDs, and more—Worldwide

For our listing of thousands of titles see our website
at
www.HeritageBooks.com

Published 2008 by
HERITAGE BOOKS, INC.
Publishing Division
100 Railroad Ave. #104
Westminster, Maryland 21157

Other books by the author:
Halsey Genealogy Since 1395 A. D.
Halsey Genealogy Since 1395 A. D., Book Two
CD: Halsey Genealogy Since 1395 A.D.

International Standard Book Numbers
Paperbound: 978-0-7884-4549-1
Clothbound: 978-0-7884-7301-2

Dedication

Dedicated to a way of life
And to all of the people whose love and guidance
have been the foundation of my life.
Each of them made a difference.

Also dedicated to Ellen, my wife and editor.

Table of Contents

**Introducing
Mom & Me
April 1935**

Introduction
"The path from cradle to grave is filled with so many perils it's a wonder that we reach the latter." Unknown

"Precious mem'ries how they linger, how they ever flood my soul; in the stillness of the midnight; precious sacred scenes unfold"- As I hum the words from the chorus of this famous old hymn, I can still hear the wavy sounds emanating from the open windows of the Pierpoint Primitive Baptist Church as the congregation's voices bounce off the mountains sending an echo into Slab Fork Hollow. Whatever motivated J.B.F. Wright to write this old hymn were probably the same thoughts and insights that we all experience as we grow old and reflect upon "home" and the events of yesteryear. This hymn represents the very first music that I can recollect hearing. Heretofore, I have developed no rhythm or musical talent, and I am not a religious person, but I have always loved listening to old time gospel music. Precious Mem'ries is one of my all time favorite hymns.

I can still hear the congregation singing "Precious Mem'ries" without musical accompaniment as the sounds vibrated inside this small church. Every song was sung, without instrumental accompaniment, with the same tempo like a roller coaster or wavy sound like reading poetry. In the hot summer months, the congregation would assemble outside under a large maple tree. Their singing would reverberate within the hollows, bouncing off the surrounding mountains. One summer in the 1940s, the funeral for one of my great aunts was held under this huge maple.

As I begin to unfold my mind's many memories of past scenes, I get a warm and fuzzy feeling. A sense of contentment comes over me as I recollect the favorite events of my most cherished and pleasant remembrances that seem to go back in time. These are "mem'ries" of scenes that appear to be as clear today as if they happened just yesterday. As I enter my 71st year, I realize that past mem'ries become more sacred.

Retirement has allowed my creative juices to continue flowing freely as I reflect on yesteryear's life within those magnificent West Virginia hills. Having visited every corner of the North American continent, I have come to believe, as others before me have, that these mountains, without question, represent the beginning and the end of all natural scenery. There is nothing as natural as a mountain stream cascading down a steep hollow creating a series of small waterfalls as the water begins its journey to the sea. Crevices of rock outcrops are decorated with mosses, herbs and ferns as the rock has stubbornly defied a millennium of erosion. The cavalcades of nature's color that adorn the mountain's outer garment in the fall create a spectacular scene, as does a

David Halsey

blanket of snow that contrast against a bluish ultraviolet winter sky. Mother Nature strategically scatters flowers of the dogwood and serviceberry trees announcing the arrival of spring in the mountains as every other tree continues to receives its wakeup call from a deep winter's sleep. A blanket of green will slowly conquer the browns of slumberhood as spring searches for summer. These are the mountains that I first observed. These are the mountains that will exist long after man is around to enjoy their splendor.

During the retirement phase of one's life, organizational constraints have evaporated allowing an engineer or scientist to experience the creative juices that flowed when careers were young. That was a time when our youthful educated ego allowed us to tackle any problem! Our thoughts and hopes are based upon what our minds have absorbed which makes us who we are. In my case, the mental recording process doesn't seem to age, but the memory retrieval system appears to have slowed down with time as my attention span gets narrower.

The recollections that I have chosen to record are about the special people and the culture in which they knowingly or unknowingly took the time to pass on their special "life's experiences" and gems of wisdom. These insights gave me a leg up on growing-up as well as clearing my path toward this thing called maturity or adulthood. The recollections recorded here are my interpretation of the wise counsel that I received from these elder folk. They blended their time with my time as they enlightened me about their individual world and its happenings have served me well. They never, once, told me how to behave but allowed me to react to whatever confronted me as I learned life's lessons. These special folk left an unforgettable image etched upon my mind even though their world and my world only met for such a brief period of time. (The only person that I can recall who gave me advice as a teenager and made me listen was a West Virginia State Trooper after I had spent a night in the Wyoming County jail (more later, maybe).)

The story that follows is like a journey up the main stem of the Ohio River. Each chapter is like a major tributary, arranged somewhat in a chronological order, written with a central theme without too many diversions, thus some of the stories do overlap. As my journey continues, particularly into the 1950s, my knowledge increases causing my world to expand at an accelerated rate.

These mem'ries have not faded into the vast emptiness of time but are the thoughts of "home" that cause great songs to endure the ages. They are mem'ries that are constantly being triggered by a longing to "go back" for one last time. This journey begins in the southern Appalachian coalfields in the mid-1930s and continues into the early 1950s. The beginning environment describes a culture that has no indoor plumbing, few have electric, and all have outdoor privies. Most folk didn't own a vehicle, and most of the roads were not paved. Some folk worked in the mines, some worked in the timber industry, and some folk just did odd jobs whenever they needed money. Almost every family practiced vegetable farming on the hill sides, hunted the mountains for meat, some raised hogs, and every teenager picked blackberries and wild grapes.

Chapters will begin with an apropos quote from a report researched and written by my youngest son, Jason David, in 1989, as a writing assignment for a project in the 7th grade at Franklin Middle School in Fairfax County, VA, entitled "David Halsey-A Biography". His thoughts certainly *flooded my soul.*

My journey is documented by the mem'ries of a time, place and folk that exist today only in my mind. A journey that can only take place growing up in an Appalachian culture where it was a *way of life* for most of our parents to quit school at age 16, regardless of the grade that they had achieved. What was most important for them, in order to function successfully within their society, was to learn the three "R's": *readin', ritin'* and *'rithmetic.* At 16 one could quit school legally, that is to say that the truant officer would not come after you. In the 30's and 40's truant officers were very active in these parts.

In the 1940s our evenings were generally family gatherings with no television or radio. This allowed bonding and spending a lot of time with our elders. We strove to accomplish things because our elders would brag on our accomplishments. Our successes were the subject of many back porch or clothesline gossip sessions, and we knew it and acted accordingly. Once we entered high school, a different kind of respect came to us, as we were treated as adults and our views, more times than not, became the center of any family gathering. We had gained some of the knowledge but not the wisdom.

From those special times together we can all recollect our elders trying, subtly, to persuade and motivate us to continue our schooling. Since most of us quickly passed our parents "book learning curve", we respected their wise counsel. I was saying "yes sir" and "no ma'am" long before I wore a military uniform. Of course, our parents embellished their comments encouraging our learning and study habits by telling us that when they went to school it was really tough. Just how tough? As a matter of fact according to them, when they went to school they had to go **uphill both ways and they made the trek barefooted in the snow!** As I get older, I realize just how valuable their foresight and advice were, from a generation that had the wisdom to want their offspring to have a life better than they had.

David Halsey

Just a simple passing moment of humming this old hymn continues to carry me back in time as a stimulus for writing my recollections in this story. My take on the *truths of the past is that they become the myths of the future, and the tales of the present*. This is my tale!

> *Precious mem'ries, unseen angels,*
> *Sent from somewhere to my soul;*
> *How they linger, ever near me,*
> *And the sacred past unfold.*
>
> *Precious father, loving mother,*
> *Fly across the lonely years;*
> *And old home scenes of my childhood*
> *In fond memory appear.*
>
> *As I travel on life's pathway,*
> *Know not what the years may hold;*
> *As I ponder, hope grows fonder,*
> *Precious mem'ries flood my soul.*
>
> *In the stillness of the midnight,*
> *Echoes from the past I hear;*
> *Old-time singing, gladness bringing,*
> *From that lovely land somewhere.*

In the Beginning

Ralph, David and Omeda Halsey,
1935

Chapter 1
In The Beginning

"David Halsey is a fun guy – an ordinary guy. He is an overachiever. He goes all out at everything in which he participates. He is never satisfied. He is always searching for new challenges. He always wants to do better himself and for everyone else he is associated with to do better also. But that is alright. He just expects everyone to do their best"- Jason David Halsey-1989

It was a Monday, traditionally called "washday" in those parts. It was about four in the morning on what happened to be April fool's Day, 1935. The scene was dark, staged in one of the two bedrooms of a small wood-framed house that rested on the side of a small hill for many years without experiencing such an event neither before nor after this one. That cottage was sitting upon locust posts and was nestled above the bottomlands on a rise that marked the entrance of a tributary into the main hollow cut by Slab Fork Creek, deep inside the southern Appalachian Mountains of West Virginia in a small coal mining town called Pierpoint. My mother was crying out experiencing birthing pains for the first time. My Grandmother Cook went about her midwifery duties of assisting her youngest daughter with her firstborn.

The house was beside a narrow dirt road that runs along the ridgeline. It was across the road from a small building that, to this day, is the meeting place for the members of the Pierpoint Primitive Baptist Church. The house did not stand the test of time as it deteriorated with age and was eventually destroyed.

One of the reasons that I happened to be born in that place is that my great-great grandfather, Henry Drury Halsey, not only brought the Halsey name to southern West Virginia in 1866, but he brought the Primitive Baptist doctrine with him. As far back as I can remember the church was always referred to as "Hard Shell" Baptist because they never cut any slack to anyone that did not adhere to the doctrine of the church. Drury was a Confederate chaplain with the rank of captain in the North Carolina militia during the War, as well as a church Elder and a circuit preacher. Over time, he established several churches in that part of Appalachia.

During his travels as a circuit preacher, Drury had befriended the Hatfield clan. As a matter of fact, his namesake, Henry Drury Hatfield, a nephew of "Devil" Anse Hatfield, was born on Mate Creek, Logan County, WV, on September 15, 1875. Henry Drury Hatfield became a medical doctor and the 14th Governor of West Virginia. The Governor was also the President of the State Senate and was the first Governor to ride in an automobile in his inaugural parade. After his term as Governor, he joined the Army Medical Corps as a surgeon for the duration of W.W.I. He died October 25, 1962.

Grandma Cook was the very first person to meet me when she pulled me from mother's womb and slapped my bottom. She and I developed a special bond that continued until she died in November 1953 at age 84. I was a freshman at Marshall College that year so she and I left home at about the same time. It was as though she stayed around until she was sure that my life would be okay. Most everyone agreed that I was Granny's favorite. She made no effort to dissuade anyone of that fact as some of my siblings often felt the sting of her crutch.

One of the most interesting things about Granny's age was that she was born in 1869 only four years after the Civil War had ended. The fact that people she knew while growing up had been in that war was always an amazing thing to me.

My mother was a tough but fragile young lady, and in her large family she was the baby. Her father had died before her 5th birthday, so her three elder brothers, Fred[1] (Uncle Fud), Dewey and James became her father figures. They spoiled her rotten. My father spent the rest of her life doing the same! When mom was 17 years old, she was in a motorcycle wreck that nearly took her life, but, in time, she recovered. Her tough-mindedness served her well as she reentered Milam High School and graduated at the age of 22 in 1933.

Mom was born Omeda Ellen Cook in a small hamlet called Hotchkiss in Raleigh County, West Virginia, located several miles further up the Slab Fork Hollow from my birthplace. Her nickname was "Oma". She was the eighth child of Minerva Birchfield and Mathew Ellison Cook. Her seven older siblings were born at a place that was located farther into the mountains. That place was called "Jinney's Gap" where Grandpa Cook and his family survived as hillside dirt farmers. Sometime after Grandpa Cook died in 1916, Grandma Cook and mom moved to a coal mining town called Glen Morrison. There they lived with one of her brothers who worked in the nearby Sabine coal mine.

The majority of the kids in that era, particularly boys, quit school after their 16th birthday, an age when they were eligible to begin working in the coal mines or on a crew harvesting timber. Most boys never advanced beyond the 8th grade, which was the top grade in most one-room schoolhouses. Students that continued their schooling attended a small high school in a nearby town called Milam. That town now has a post office and is called McGraws.

After graduation from high school with 10 classmates, mom moved to the "big" town of Pierpoint, population of about 100 folk, to

---

[1] Uncle Fred (Fud) did not know until he entered the Army in 1917 that his real name was not Fred nor Fud but Steve Wilbur Cook! Nicknames and misspelling proper names were common occurrences in Appalachia. It drove the census takers crazy and compounded their errors. I didn't know until after I was commissioned into the Army that my middle name was spelled "Herald" on my birth certificate. Then and now I spell it "Harold".

stay with her first cousin's widow, Loutisa Sparks Birchfield. That tradition continued during my teen years, as cousins born and reared in the "boondocks" stayed with us in "town". That move improved their chances of finding a husband or wife that was not their cousin. That is how my mom met my father, Ralph Halsey, who was born and grew up in Pierpoint about 100 yards from Loutisa's house.

Loutisa Birchfield eventually married Herbert Morgan, dad's first cousin and lifelong close friend. As time would tell, I became the nearest thing to Loutisa's having a child of her own. Because of that, she was always looking after my best interests. As I grew older, I referred to her as my Aunt Loutisa. She was my high school English teacher, and whatever I did was okay with her, up to a point. I made good grades in English without learning much about grammar. She would ask, "David, do you understand your English assignment?" I would reply, "Yes ma'am. I have some of it done already." She would say, "Okay. You give it to me when you finish." Many times I never turned in any work. Years later when I entered Marshall College, I tested so poorly in English grammar that I was assigned to what was commonly called "bonehead" English. I had to attend English grammar classes five days a week for a year.

Aunt Loutisa was a tall, handsome lady whose appearance was always immaculate. However, she did have one bad habit. She dipped snuff, and, by the end of a school day, the tobacco juice ran from her mouth down her chin into her wrinkles. She started the first Sunday school in that small settlement of Pierpoint. In the mid-1980's, long after she had retired from a long and distinguished teaching career at a time when I was winding down my engineering career, she became my inspiration and motivation for membership in the Mullens High School Area Hall of Fame. Unfortunately, she and dad both died before I was inducted.

Dad was the oldest of seven siblings. He lost his mother, Sarah Elizabeth Lambert Halsey, in 1928 when he was only 19. His father, Elijah Coy Halsey, had lost part of his right leg in the mines and was unable to support the family so dad took on that responsibility. He started working in the coal mines the same year his mother died.

So the baby daughter of a large fatherless family, good looking, unmarried at age 22, met her "knight in shining armor" who was 25 years old at that juncture. He had been responsible for raising his six siblings for about six years. They fell in love, and the Reverend Mullins married them in Mullens, the largest city in the county, on May 12, 1934. Mullens was named after the preacher's family with a slight misspelling probably caused by bad handwriting. It is located about five miles from my birthplace, at the mouth of the hollow where Slab Fork Creek empties into the great Guyandotte River.

Granny Cook always lived with us. When I was about five or six years old, Granny frequently visited her other children and took me along. We walked up the hollow about one mile from Pierpoint to the Maben train depot to catch the train. The Virginian's steam passenger train took us about 10 miles further up the hollow to a coal camp called Slab Fork. From there we walked a few miles to the top of Acord Mountain to visit her daughter, Mary Frances, and family. Sometimes we stayed on the train until the next station, called Lester, where we walked a few miles to a place called "Maple Meadow". At that time Granny's three sons, Fred, Dewey and James, had moved their families to Maple Meadow. I can still hear the old conductor as he walked through the car calling out "Lusssster, Lusssster, next stop Lusssster". Once or twice we walked from Maple Meadow to Acord Mountain which took most of the day. I still can remember getting really thirsty, taking a cool drink of water from a spring-fed branch, and how good it tasted.

Grandma Cook chewed Brown's Mule tobacco that she carved from a "plug" using a small Case pocketknife. The main blade was almost worn through. Occasionally, she smoked a corncob pipe. She was the only grandparent that I ever knew. My Grandpa Halsey got to meet me and probably held me, but I don't remember him since he died on Christmas Eve in 1936. My Aunt Irene told me years later that at his wake she remembers me crawling in and around his pine box coffin, which was resting on two kitchen chairs in his house.

The Halsey family has been settled in America since 1633. Dad represented the fourth generation in Wyoming County, WV, the twelfth generation in America, and the sixteenth generation of known direct lineage.[2] His maternal Grandmother's ancestors (her name was Cathany Sizemore Halsey) had been in America a little longer since they were direct descendants of Eastern Cherokee Indians.

My father was the last of my family's lineage to spend his entire life living in West Virginia. He never lived more than a couple miles from his birthplace. A month or so after I was born, mom, dad and I moved to a brand new house located about two miles down the hollow from Pierpoint in a coal mining town called Otsego.

---

[2] The Halsey lineage is presented in my book; "HALSEY GENEALOGY SINCE 1395", Heritage Books, Bowie MD, 1995

An Appalachian Coal Camp

Otsego, Wyoming County, West Virginia
circa 1938

Chapter 2
An Appalachian Coal Camp

"The family did not have indoor plumbing until David was away at college.
They had a radio that worked on a battery; they saved the battery for Saturday's so that
they could listen to the Grand Ole Opry. They did not have a TV and David was 12 before
they had a car." Jason David Halsey, 1989

Recently, I walked into Otsego coal camp traveling up its only street passing the overgrown vacant lot, which was once the community playground, toward where the company store, shop, bathhouse and mines used to be located. That was just across from what used to be the Virginian but is now the Norfolk and Western Railroad tracks. Memories that fill in the details of what it was like 60+ years ago raced through my mind.

I suspect that Otsego was probably more like other coal camps rather than different, however, the special combination of people and mine operators bonded into an entity that produced a camaraderie that still survives among the miners' offspring. When we have our Mullens High School graduating class reunions (my 51st was held in 2004), recognition is always afforded to those of us who were raised in and around a coal camp emphasizing a distinction from chaps raised in Mullens town proper.

The chance any kid had to grow up in a coal camp lasted from the early 1930's to the mid- 50's. Otsego went from a boomtown to a sleepy little settlement in about 25 years' time, existing for merely one generation - mine! I was born in '35 which was about a year before the coal mine at Otsego was deemed to be the most mechanized operation that existed anywhere. According to the "Oglebay Norton Company's-125 years 1854-1979" publication, in 1936, the company managed the Brule Mine in West Virginia. It was the nation's first completely mechanized coal mine. Erin Coal Company was the original developer of the Otsego mines, and data shows the Erin mines produced 40,661 tons of coal in 1933, their last year of operation before the takeover by Oglebay.

Sometime during the summer of '35, mom, dad and I moved into our first new home at Otsego. It was the third house up the street from the superintendent's house. My brother Richard and sisters, Edna and Margaret, were subsequently born in that house. It's one of the few still standing today. What remains today are a few old company houses that individuals have remodeled somewhat but not enough to change their character, a church, ruins of the old bathhouse, company store, mines and tipple.

Otsego was built upon the bottoms formed by Cedar Creek's entrance into Slab Fork Creek. Slab Fork is a major tributary to the Great Guyandotte River that flows into the mighty Ohio at Guyandotte near Huntington, WV. Slab Fork Creek, still untouched by pollution at that time, was teeming with aquatic life. Small mouth and rock bass, commonly called "redeye's", aggressively hit a hellgrammite or crawdad dangling from an angler's hook.

As I became engrossed in the research for my books on genealogy, I discovered that this land was cleared by one of my paternal great-great-grandfathers, Franklin Sizemore, who was close to being a full-blooded Cherokee Indian. He built a one-room cabin on the large bottomlands near the mouth of Cedar Creek. In 1874, he added a room to his cabin and in it taught the first term of public school in that area. Class size ranged from eight to twelve students. The first public schoolhouse in that area was built near the Sizemore home in 1880. During that same year, he established a post office that he called "Cedarsburg". Cedarsburg was eventually renamed Otsego. Sizemore was its first postmaster. Cedarsburg was on the fifth postal route that was established in Wyoming County, southern West Virginia. It ran between Pineville, the county seat, to Beckley, the county seat of Raleigh Co., along a route marked by post offices at Newfound, Saulsville, and Cedarsburg. The mail was carried on horseback with two weekly round trips. James Sauls (Saulsville) was the first carrier. Peter Snuffer was the second, and James Remley Cook, one of my maternal great-grandfathers, was the third carrier. My ancestors did their part in laying the groundwork for future generations.

The only street was unpaved except by coal dust commonly called fines that had fallen from overloaded dump trucks making local deliveries. A whitewashed board fence that ran down both sides marked the street's boundary. The fence protected fairly new wood-framed houses that lined both sides of the street. All were freshly painted white and were accessible by a gate in front of each house. Each house was a clone of the others. They stood like soldiers frozen in formation.

Over the winter months, numerous potholes formed in the street. They were caused by water from rain and snow, freezing and thawing, coupled with the constant pounding of loaded coal trucks. Whenever the superintendent decided spring weather had arrived, the utility men, who were responsible for the appearance of the camp, filled up the potholes with material that appeared to be half coal and half soil. That was before ash was available from the burning slag pile. As summer approached, the street began to dry up leaving a thin layer of coal dust clinging to every blade of grass, the wooden fences, front porches, and everything else that was close to the street. The color tones faded from black on the fence's bottom board nearest the street to grayish white on the front porches of the houses.

The company's mine operation buildings were constructed with cinder blocks and also painted white. In general, the coal camp was situated in a lineal fashion because of the V-shaped valley. There was only room for a street, two rows of houses, Slab Fork Creek and one set of railroad tracks. In Otsego, the superintendent's house was located in the most convenient spot away from the traffic generated by the mine and company store.

The railroad and trains played a large part in our daily lives. I can remember the many times that we stood under the overhang that protected the entrance to the mine office and post office. It was located in a small section attached to the larger Brule Smokeless Coal Company's store. We stood there in anticipation of the arrival of Virginian Railroad's passenger train "No. 3". Each day at about the same time the westbound train, consisting of an engine with water tender and two passenger cars trailing a baggage car, arrived on its trek from Roanoke, Virginia, through southern West Virginia to Deepwater in Kanawha County near the State Capital of Charleston. Long before the iron-nosed cow catcher of the "Pacific No. 210" engine appeared from the Otsego Tunnel, you could hear the whistle sounds echo amidst the hills. The engineer pulled the steam cord with a rhythmic motion that was his signature as the passenger train passed over the Caloric and Newriva crossings up the Slab Fork Hollow a few miles just above the town of Mullens. Those small, relatively fast locomotives were equipped with whistles that had a higher frequency than the lower pitched whistles of the larger locomotives that pulled the coal trains. From where we were standing, the tunnel entrance was only a few hundred feet away. As the train approached, the air was filled with a subtle aroma of steam, smoke and hot lubricant. A gentle breeze made the smells stronger as the engine pushed its way out of the tunnel onto the bridge. The air brakes squeaked as the train slowed to a stop. The relaxed steam engine began to belch black smoke full of cinders from its stack. Steam was released through the gage relief valve to rid the boilers of excess pressure as the engine relaxed for the short rest at the Otsego whistle stop.

From our vantage point, the rails were just a few feet across the "reddog" road, so you could feel the earth vibrate and hear the steam engine pulsating as "No. 3" crossed the bridge braking to a stop directly in front of us. Since the engineer and fireman always kept a full head of steam, there was always a pulsating thud as if the engine was catching its breath as excess steam was being released. Depending upon the wind direction, you could get an eye full of cinders if the fireman decided to shovel coal into the furnace. A short time later, a twin train, "No. 4" arrived going eastbound toward Norfolk, VA.

The arrival of those passenger trains was a daily happening. They were our transportation down the hollow to the city of Mullens three miles away and in the other direction to our kinfolk living on Acord Mountain near the Slab Fork station and on Maple Meadow near the Lester stop. All were nestled deep in the southern Appalachian mountains of West Virginia. The Virginian's passenger service faded out after WWII as the highway systems and automobiles improved.

According to "An Introduction to the Virginian Railway" by Martin E. Swartz of The Norfolk and Western Historical Society, the

Virginian was the creation of one man, Henry Huttleston Rogers of New York. His Tidewater railroad merged with William Page's Deepwater railroad in 1907. Rogers died in 1909, the year of my father's birth. Mark Twain, a close personal friend of Rogers, was one of his pallbearers. Twain attended the dedication of the Virginian the year before but chose not to make the railroad's inaugural trip across the mountains with Rogers.

After the rails were laid on a grade carved along the Slab Fork Creek upstream from Mullens on the way to Deepwater, Kanawha County, WV, the coalmining era began. Somewhere in this beginning, the die was cast for Cedarsburg to emerge as Otsego, "the coal camp". The "richest little railroad in the world", the Virginian was ready to haul Otsego's high grade metallurgical coal 446 miles to the seaport of Newport News for delivery to worldwide markets. The railroad completion to Deepwater provided the connection to serve major U.S. markets. The large cities craved the smokeless, high-energy, metallurgical coal that contains the least amount of ash and the most calories (energy) per pound of any coal in the world.

The Virginian was generally on the edge of technology in the development of new large steam locomotives. During the 1940's, the 800 series, one of the largest steam locomotives produced in the world, was put into service to pull mile-long coal trains over steep grades that snaked through those Appalachian Mountains. I can remember seeing coal "drags", as a coal train was called, with two engines in front and a "pusher" in the rear. Each railroad car's wheels on the outside of a curve made a high pitched screeching sound as the many curves were negotiated. Local lore suggests that the railroad surveyors were "akin" to a snake. Each car wheel had an oil box that contained a stringy cotton material soaked in thick oil to keep lubricant on the wheel axle. Sometimes after dark as a train passed, you could see the red hot glow of a wheel oil box as it was running out of oil. We also learned early in life that you didn't want to be standing under a bridge when those large engines crossed because the hot "rain" that fell on you was steam a few seconds earlier.

Echoes from the sounds of so many different locomotive whistles that were played so distinctly by each engineer are still vivid in my mind. Many songs have been written in an attempt to capture the "lonesome" mystical mood caused by the sound of a steam locomotive's whistle as it echoed in those deep hollows. Only the purist railroad enthusiast could identify the engineers by their whistle sounds. I was a fortunate kid to have witnessed such a piece of Americana. I learned later after my first physics class about how the "Doppler" effect caused the whistle tones to have a higher pitch as the engine came toward us and a lower pitch as the engine went off into the distance.

Every mine operation developed a slate or refuse pile. Since a seam of coal is almost never level and never a consistent thickness, the mineshaft is like a line on a piece of wavy paper, similar to a small roller coaster. The mining operation needs to maintain a minimum ceiling height to provide clearance for men and machines. Thus, the mining operation produced, in addition to coal, lots of rock and slate. In the coal fields, slate is commonly called "bone". Therefore, the slag or refuse pile became known as the "bone" pile.

At Otsego the debris from the processing plant, called a tipple, was delivered to the slag pile by an aerial tram. For balance and efficiency the tram had two large cars, called buckets, equally spaced so that when one was loading at the tipple, the other one was dumping at the slag pile. As I recall, the buckets had wheels that ran on separate pairs of cables from the tipple to a large hollow about one-half mile away. The location of the slag pile was chosen so that the pile had enough room to expand since it had to serve the life of the mine operations. As the refuse pile becomes bigger, its weight, pressure and the energy contained in the discarded coal will eventually cause it to catch fire due to spontaneous combustion. The ash that is produced is reddish–gray in color, thus called "reddog". That burnt material makes an excellent road topping treatment. Also, the burning slag pile produces hydrogen sulfide and carbon monoxide, both very deadly gases if inhaled in high concentrations. Small concentrations of sulfur in the smoke from the burning slag pile caused the lead paint on the company's white houses and any other houses for a mile or two up and down the hollow to turn black over time. Most white paint during that era contained some amount of lead.

During the winters of the 1930's and 40's, the "hobo years", transient hobos slept next to the visible flame or warm glow of the slag pile. If the breezes were just right, they never woke up due to the poisonous gases. In any case, you can almost be assured that each survivor had a terrific headache the next day. I can recall the grownups talking about burying several hobos during that time.

I remember the hot showers that we took as youngsters at the mine bathhouse, which was built after World War II (WWII). It was our first experience with indoor plumbing. We stood under those hot showers, holding on to the chain, for what seemed to be an eternity, until our bodies were wrinkled like a prune. Some of us were too small to reach the shower chains, so the taller boys tied the chains so the showers were open.

Our basketball rims and sled runners were made and repaired at the mine machine shop. There were many evenings where "knowledge" was gleaned from conversations that took place around the potbellied stove at the company store during the short days of a long cold Appalachian winter. As part of my "after school education", that was where I first learned about FDR, John L. Lewis, coal mining techniques, politics and religion from a coal miner's viewpoint. I also learned how to chew tobacco and the technique of spitting on the red hot spot of the potbelly stove that caused the spit to ricochet and not stick. Almost every miner chewed tobacco since it was illegal to smoke inside a mine. We had a steady supply of chewing tobacco from searching our dad's work clothes before mom washed them. We usually found several opened pouches that contained a chew or two in dad's two layers of clothing that were worn underground since it was always near 56 degrees inside the mine, year-round.

One of my favorite places in Otsego was "the vacant lot" which was just across the street from our house. Some of my fondest memories and scariest moments are related to that lot which was part of my adolescent world. During the Christmas season, a large community tree was erected and decorated on the lot. If the weather cooperated, Santa Claus, from the bed of a large truck, passed out presents to each child. All of the miners' children received major gifts, plus ample candy and fruit and nuts for the entire family. If the weather didn't cooperate, we all gathered inside the Union Hall at Caloric about a mile downstream from Otsego. I remember how crowded it was, but no one minded. My brother Richard and I would stand holding on to dad's legs awaiting the arrival of Santa. Santa always showed up with a truckload of gifts. The vacant lot was also one of the places where all the males gathered on Sunday afternoons to shoot marbles.

Late one summer day when I was about five or so, I was playing on the vacant lot, running to and fro when all of a sudden the ground began to give way. I slowly sank into the ground. An opossum ran from a hole in front of me obviously disturbed by the sudden intrusion. I was barefooted and wearing shorts and I felt several hard objects rub my feet and legs as I sank. The ground had swallowed my legs up to my crotch! Later, I learned what it was that felt so cold and damp. It was the entrails of a horse that had been buried in a shallow grave in the far corner of the lot a few weeks before. I can still vividly feel those rib bones rub my legs as my feet slowly sank in between them!

One year later, 1940, after we moved back to nearby Pierpoint to a house that was built by dad and his Uncle Ike, I learned that the horse was the same one that the "paperboy" rode each week when he delivered the "Grit" newspaper. I remember watching him lazily ride up the street with his leg draped across the saddle so he could doze or pretend to doze to fool us. You had to be alert because his favorite pastime was to use us kids as targets when he delivered the paper. Since each porch was only 5 or 6 feet from the board fence, we were easy targets. There was not much room in the front yard for flowers. However, at a house up from ours toward the company store, a lady had planted some type of flowers that the horse seemed to like. As the horse passed her house, he would stop and take a bite. The paperboy was not too attentive. The lady's husband decided to "shock" the horse so he would leave the flowers alone. As I was later told, he laid a wire along the top board of the fence, near the flowers, and attached the wire to the house current. I also learned that you could prevent the fuse from blowing if you put a penny behind it. The current electrocuted the horse and shocked the paperboy. I finally knew why the paperboy and horse didn't come around anymore.

On the Fourth of July by mid-morning, folk assembled on the grounds of the Otsego School. Some family names that I recall are the Marshalls, Stonemans, Meadows, Van Camps, Sarvers, Jenkins, Cooks, O'Dells, Yates, Lewis, Whitts, Rhineharts, Lambonis, Bakers, Hiltons, Franaus and many, many more. As people gathered, the "Que Bee" (later to be Sunbeam) bread, cake and pie as well as the "Southern Maid" (now Foremost) ice cream trucks arrived compliments of the Brule Smokeless Coal Company. Clyde Acord's band consisting of guitar, fiddle and mandolin players entertained with Clyde harmonizing with others as they stood under a large oak tree in the schoolyard. He was a local musician as well as a coal miner. Picnic tables were placed nearby to take advantage of the shade from the same huge oak. Tables were made from the same rough cut sawmill green lumber as the mine timbers and cribbing logs. An adult kept us at bay and in line, as we waited in anticipation of all the cake and ice cream that we could eat. That was a tough problem for us. Needless to say, we kids would "glut" ourselves from eating too much.

Labor Day celebrations were just as elaborate as those on the Fourth of July. Normally, the gathering was held at a ball field in nearby Caloric. Otsego had an employee baseball team that played a doubleheader with a club from another camp or a town like Mullens. Sometimes extra innings were played when some pitcher challenged the opposing batters.

Other entertainment was the competition between mine rescue teams. Most coal mining operations had several rescue teams consisting of trained individuals skilled in mine rescue operations, such as first aide and fire, smoke, and cave-in recovery, explosions, etc. The competition involved a simulated mine emergency or injured miner scenario. Each team's members performed certain designated tasks, for example, preparing an injured miner for evacuation from the mine. Teams were dressed in distinct coveralls or uniforms with name and company logo and were judged by time and quality of their efforts. Folks from the camp voiced their encouragement and cheer for the home team but recognized and respected the efforts of the visiting team. Everyone, even us kids, realized the importance of their talents and bravery since we all had seen and lived through mine disasters. We had all experienced that unexplainable empty and scary feeling when the mine whistle didn't stop sounding. I can remember the heartache after a mine explosion killed several miners. Everyone knew each other as friends and neighbors. Almost without exception, every mine disaster meant death.

At 19 years old, dad had gone to work at Otsego in 1928, shortly after his mother died in June of that year. Erin Smokeless Coal Company was the operator at that time. By 1936 pop had seen the good, bad and punishing misery of mining coal in one of the more than twenty minable seams that were layered like an old fashioned molasses layered cake inside the mountain. Coal in each seam ranged in thickness from about thirty inches to about fifty inches. The seam at the Otsego drift mine location was about three feet thick. He learned to do virtually every job and chore that needed to be done to mine coal. With barely an eighth-grade education in a two-room school at nearby Pierpoint, dad was as industrious, dependable and reliable as a person could be, always looking to improve and to excel. His word was his bond. During his career of 23 years at Otsego, he was part of a mining mechanization revolution, participating as it went from a "pick and shovel" operation to the nation's most modern mechanized coal mine. He continued his professional and personal growth eventually becoming a mine foreman. I remember as a 10-year-old spending many winter nights watching dad disassemble and reassemble the miner's safety light in preparation for the "fire boss"[3] test and certification. I learned to do it also. Coal dust and methane gas are the major fuels that cause mine explosions.

Since the mining company owned the town, you could only live there if you worked for them. As I remember, the folk living in Otsego bonded very tightly. That is to say that whenever a miner's son reached his 18th birthday, he could have a job with the company. If he chose to go underground, he needed a sponsor or mentor, such as his dad, uncle, older brother, or a close neighbor. Someone had to take responsibility for teaching the rookie how to become a coal miner and to prepare for his miner certification after one year. At Otsego new miners needed to learn the proper technique for mounting and dismounting a traveling belt, which was the only way into and out of the mine. There was not very much room on top of a belt full of coal because of the low ceilings coupled with timbers and cribbing to support the roof. Most of the time the trip inside was the easiest since the belt was normally stopped so supplies could be loaded. Rookies needed to learn how to position the burlap curtain to direct the air toward the mine face to accomplish proper ventilation; how to load and set the "airdox" devices (Otsego used compressed air to "shoot" the coal); and, how to spread rock dust (lime) everywhere to subdue the chances for a coal dust explosion. Plus, newcomers had to tote the mine supplies, help reposition the belts at the mine "face", and everything else a laborer was required to do. After a year of probation, each rookie miner got an opportunity to learn the operation of whatever machinery for which he had an inclination. Names like Link Belt, Jeffrey, Joy and Cardox were familiar to the young men employed at Otsego.

In January 1937 my younger brother, Richard, was born and joined us in the company house. Dad was making decent wages for that period. An example of one of his statements indicated that he got check

---

[3] A "fire boss" is the guy that travels the entire active mine sections between shifts to insure its safety for the miners.

number 62 for pay period ending September 30, 1937. He had labored for 70 hours at .9143 per hour which amounted to $64.00. However, dad's deductions were: owed to the company store: $26; for powder supplies: $8; house coal: $1.25; electric: $1; rent: $5.87; union dues: $ .50; miner's lamp: $ .80; family doctor: $ .85; hospital: $ .50; old age tax: $ .63; and, transfer coal: $1. That was a total of $46.40 deductions from his check which left him $17.60 take home pay. Contrasting this amount with the changes that WWII brought ten years later, his Christmas bonus was $250, which in itself was a large sum in 1947.

By the mid '30's, dad had emerged as a natural leader, leading by example without boasting. So naturally, he became involved in the United Mine Workers of America Union local leadership. On December 28, 1937, dad was elected to represent Local 6195, District Number 17, United Mine Workers of America, at the Thirty-fifth Consecutive Constitutional Convention. He was presented with a certificate of "Credential to the Convention" to Washington, D.C., on Tuesday, January 25, 1938.

He made the trip and was awed by his first excursion outside his birthplace in nearby Pierpoint. While in Washington, D.C., he wrote two letters to his wife, Omeda, and sons. Each letter was very descriptive of his adventure. The first letter told about the happenings at the convention. He also talked about the cold weather, probably reacting to the higher humidity and the wind chill typical for January in D.C. Also, the letter contained a comment about souvenirs. (I still have most of them.) One observation he made was that people in D.C. slept during the day and not at night. There must have been a lot of paper passed out at the convention because he made a comment about filling his suitcase.

In his second letter, he talked about some adventures that he had time for such as walking 33 blocks to visit the Smithsonian Institution National Zoo. Dad indicated that he was "amazed at what critters" he had seen. His wish was that mom and my brother, Richard, and I could have seen "every creature that you could imagine", including a turtle that weighed 300 plus pounds and a 30-foot long snake. They were huge critters compared to the snapping turtles and water snakes back home in Slab Fork Creek! He said to tell Uncle Dewey Cook, mom's older brother, that he saw a white deer. He spent more than six hours at the National Zoo. His letter ended as did the first; "tell the chaps good night for daddy, your loving dad, Ralph". He arrived back home in Otsego several days later and never again separated himself from his family. That was the only occasion on which he had reason to write letters, and those were the only two letters he ever wrote!

The summer after completing sixth grade, I got to attend a two-week nature camp at Oglebay Park near Wheeling, WV, which was a long way from Otsego. We met the company bus at the appointed time with baggage in hand and started an all day trek north to Camp Russell at Oglebay Park. There we had the best learning experience of our lives.

Bird walks before breakfast, arts and crafts before lunch, games, sports and swimming before dinner, and campfires and astronomy, which hooked me, before bedtime. The camp lasted for two weeks. Every company dependent from sixth grade through ninth grade was eligible to attend the nature camp for two years for free. Dad paid for my third year.

That way of life was homogenous and appeared to be immune from significant influences from the outside world, except when the young men returned home from defending our flag in far away places. Upon their return, changes due to a way of life learned in cultures in foreign lands had a subtle effect upon the way life was played out in that small coal camp settlement and surrounding communities nestled near the heart of the southern Appalachians. They added new words to our slang expressions and names of places to our vocabulary. That environment became more susceptible to change when the mobility and information blitz periods arrived in the 50s, thanks to the automobile and television. By that time, it was too late for Otsego. As a coal camp it was old. The mine, the very heart, was soon to close and most of the contiguous structures were torn down for scrap. The mining camp just faded away.

As I walked across the stage of the Mullens High School auditorium in '53 with diploma in hand, one of my favorite teachers, the late Mrs. Madge Kaman, who taught us all how to release all those magnificent chemistry mysteries, handed me an envelope as I started to step off the stage. She said to protect it because it was valuable. As I sat down in the seats reserved for graduates, I opened the envelope and discovered that I had been given a four-year scholarship, a "full ride", to any school that I chose, no obligations, compliments of the Brule Smokeless Coal Company and the parent company, the Oglebay Norton Corporation. Mr. Davis, the treasurer for the Peoples Bank of Mullens at the time, wrote the letter and was the custodian of the scholarship. That was how I made my exit from a once grand but aged coal camp environment.

An Otsego coal camp employee was a factor in my college choice. Carl York, a Mullens native and a star basketball player for Marshall College from 1950-54, had worked at Otsego during the summer. Carl was our "hero", so naturally I wanted to attend "his" college. I enjoyed seeing him practice his skills for the great Hall of Fame Coach Cam Henderson during his senior year.

I frequently have occasion to talk to folks who share memories of those days in Otsego. During the winter of 1988, I spent a considerable amount of time at McDill Air Force Base as a member of the U.S. Central Command team preparing the Civil Affairs contingency plans for the Middle East. My dad's second youngest sister, Irene, spent her winters with their youngest sister, Athlene, and her husband, Uncle Bill, in nearby Orange County, Florida, about two hours from McDill. During one of my McDill visits, I spent some time visiting them. Aunt Irene fixed me a meal that reminded me of "home". It consisted of pork chops and fried potatoes with onions. As I sat there in my military uniform with my "bird" colonel eagle shining, she told me about the times that she baby sat for me at Otsego. She told me stories that I had never heard before. During that time she had married a coal miner named Dallas Texas Thompson, Uncle Dal, in the fall of 1937. While the miners worked she spent a lot of time at our house. Aunt Irene was amused when reminiscing about her smoking habits during those Otsego days. She said that at that time she still did not smoke in front of her big brother, my dad.

By the time I became a teenager, I knew basically how a coal mine worked. I knew how to draw and read the mine maps; how to process and load coal into a rail car; and, how the carbide chemical process in an acid battery worked to power the miner's head light as well as the lights used in the railroad switch signals. I knew how to arc weld a broken basketball rim and sled runner and how to splice a coal mine belt that served as transportation for coal and miners into and out of the mine.

As an offspring of a coal miner, I was fortunate to receive the many benefits and blessings that were provided to us without having to risk life and limb mining coal a mile or two inside a mountain as my father and his father did before him. My parents' dreams for all of us were to find a safer life away from the heartache and physical punishment that awaited all coal miners. As a teenager, I knew that there was a bigger world out there from the many stories that guys told upon their return home from WWII. My dreams always took me far away from the prospect of becoming a coal miner. There was nothing about the mines that appealed to me. I simply wanted to see what was on the other side of the mountains!

Today the main route, Route 54, bypasses what's left of the camp going across a bridge above the railroad near where the company store once stood. That main route from Mullens to Beckley now meanders through the valley. The old road crossed Pierpoint Mountain coming down the steep slope toward the bridge across Cedar Creek near the entrance to Otsego. There was always only one road into and out of Otsego.

One-Room School

Loutisa Sparks Morgan

Pierpoint School 1925

Chapter 3
One-Room School

"From the first through the third grades, David attended a one-room school in Pierpoint. One teacher taught eight grades. Sometimes the seventh and eighth graders would teach the lower grades. This was done because most kids dropped out by the eighth grade, and the teacher didn't have time to work with any seventh and eighth who were left. There were only 15 children in the entire school." Jason David Halsey 1989

My first attempt at attending school occurred at the age of five. It was short-lived since the teacher, Mrs. Delp, sent me home because I wouldn't quit trying to whistle. I didn't return to school until the next year. Even today, I believe that early on a foggy morning I could walk up Cedar Creek toward the old schoolhouse and imagine hearing (Mrs. Effie) "Granny" Delp's school bell reverberating among those magnificent West Virginia hills.

As I entered the first grade at age six, I was finally getting a chance to begin doing things like all the older kids. Early on I had an eagerness to learn everything about everything. My first few days began with the teacher, Mrs. L. T. Lail, slapping my left hand while telling me that I had to be "normal" and write with my right hand. One reason she gave was that the wooden chair/desk was designed with an arm on the right side only, so writing was only convenient for students who were right handed. In order to write left handed, one had to position his/her left hand and write upside down as he curled his left hand around toward his right side to reach the desk. So I became ambidextrous and didn't know it. The next calamitous event that I had to contend with involved my being afraid to ask permission to go to the outhouse. The wooden chair/desk had a seat carved out so they were somewhat contoured to fit your bottom. If you peed in your pants, the fluid would stay in your seat soaking your bottom parts, which made for a long day. After this happened to me, I remember that my mom had to take me back to school the next day because I didn't want to go.

When a group of children were congregated in one room, closed in a very dry environment due to coal heat during winter months, the contagious diseases began their cycles. During my first three or so school years, I contracted the measles, mumps, whooping cough, lice and "fall" sores. The sores lasted for weeks and were treated with a deep purple-colored lotion. To eliminate lice, all the boys had "burr" haircuts. Sometimes during the winter months, we had worms. As disgusting as that sounds now, it was not uncommon then. Once the adults became aware of the worms, Granny Cook mixed a concoction of herbs and made us drink it. That potion was the worst-tasting stuff that I can ever remember ingesting, but it always worked. It seemed that every time we became ill in the wintertime, the favored cure was a laxative of some sort. The rest of those ailments had to be allowed to run their course.

From the time I received my first report card, I was impressed with Mrs. Lail's penmanship, particularly the way she signed her name, "Mrs. L.T. Lail". Her handwriting had a beautiful flowing mixture of old English font and alternating thickness and narrowing of the line from the variable pressure as she stroked her fountain pen to create those perfect letters.

One of my heroes and lifelong friends has been a cousin named Carroll "Kodge" Halsey. Kodge was a few grades ahead of me at the one-room schoolhouse in Pierpoint. He and a guy named Elwood McBride played rather roughly during recess. Mrs. Lail ordered them not to participate in wrestling matches. She punished them for disobeying her orders. It didn't take me long to become part of that male ritual. Once caught, we were punished with extra chores such as fetching twigs, small hickory limbs, for the teacher to use as switches with which she swat us. Also, we had to fetch the drinking water from a branch of the creek flowing in a nearby hollow. Another chore we had to perform was to sweep out the school and, in the winter, to cut firewood for the stove. That meant that we had to arrive early and leave late. That is where I received my first lesson in duty and responsibility in addition to learning the three R's, "readn' ", "ritin' ", and "rithmetic". The Pierpoint School was closed in the spring of 1943 by which time I was in the fourth grade and was bussed to Maben.

Schoolin' with Indoor Plumbin'....

Author is center top row.

Chapter 4
Schoolin', Knighthood, Elections, Moonshinin' & Mortality

"For the fourth through the eighth grades, he went to school in Maben, WV that had about seven rooms and was the first place he had been that had indoor plumbing and hot lunches. It was the first place where he ever took a hot shower."

"David seems to have loved school because he felt there was so much to learn and everyday there was something new. He spent most of his free time in the library reading books trying to learn as much as he could. The library was in the principal's office."

"The typical school day for David would be to get up early and ride a bus to school on winding mountain roads. When he got to school, the teacher would ring a bell on the front porch and have the children line up for roll call; from there they went to their classes" Jason David Halsey 1989

My educational world exploded beginning with the very first day that I got aboard the school bus in late summer of 1943 to attend school in nearby Maben. The Maben School was built in 1926 by the William N. Ritter Lumber Company and functioned as a high school for many years. By the way, for the next nine years, my schools were the only buildings in which I spent time that had indoor plumbing.

From my very first day in the fourth grade, I felt very motivated. As we stepped from the school bus, a teacher rang a bell, and all the chaps formed a line standing shoulder-to-shoulder facing the school. The line closest to the school consisted of first graders, while the eighth graders were the last in line. The first day I quickly found my place in the fourth row. It was a good feeling to have three rows of younger kids in front of me.

My Aunt Beatrice, whom we called "Ant Beet", was one of the school cooks. I do remember some of her delicious hot meals, particularly her burnt meat loaf with mashed potatoes and creamed peas. That meal, as well as salmon croquettes, is still one of my favorite meals.

The janitor was a neighbor from Pierpoint who was also a shoe cobbler. He had lost a leg in his younger life, probably caused by an accident either inside a coal mine or working on the railroad. I never thought to ask him about the missing leg since it was normal for us to see him walk with a wooden peg leg. His name was Charlie McGraw, and we all called him "Uncle Charlie". If I was to choose one of the first people who inspired my interest in engineering, it would be Uncle Charlie. From the onset he called me "King David", of course, from the biblical reference.

The school had a coal-fired boiler that produced steam that was piped to cast iron radiators in each room to provide heat. I spent a lot of time with Uncle Charlie as he took the time to explain in detail and answer all my questions about how the furnace, boiler and radiators functioned. That was my first lesson in thermodynamics given by a man that may have finished at the most five or six grades of formal education.

During each spring one of the county grade schools took its turn as host for what was called the "Annual Festival". The festival can best be described as an Olympic-like event consisting of academic and athletic competition. During the morning session, two or three individuals from each grade of the participating schools took tests in math, English, social studies, etc., to see who scored the highest by answering the most questions correctly. Each grade's score sheet was tallied, and the winners received a certificate of merit for the particular event in which they did well.

In the afternoon, individual athletic events took place, such as throwing a ball, broad jump, sprint races, etc. Certificates were also awarded to those winners. One thing that I remember about the competition is that we had a girl who could throw a ball farther than any eighth-grade boy. She represented our school. We rooted for her, but it hurt the boys' pride big time.

By the time I had made it to the eighth grade level, I thought that taking any test was fun, and I always looked forward to any competition that involved testing one's knowledge. That attitude served me well when I went to college.

Maben School was housed in a two-story brick building with a basement, but the gymnasium was a detached wooden building. In the wintertime the gym was heated by a potbellied stove, and, since there was no insulation, all the warmth was near the potbellied stove. Whenever a basketball game or dance was concluded all the people huddled around the stove for warmth. Even during timeouts at winter basketball games, both the players and some of the parents took advantage of the timeouts to find a little warmth.

The gym also served as the "community building". As such, popular fundraising events like "cakewalks" were held. For a cakewalk, ladies baked a variety of cakes, and, as music was being played, a line of prepaid folk marched single file around the gym floor passing a designated point. When the music stopped, someone dropped a broom in front of the person who had reached that point, and he/she won a cake. I remember a very young duo named Everett and Bea Lilly from Beckley playing what was to become Bluegrass music at one of the cakewalks. By the way, I listen to Bluegrass music on Cirrus radio via Dish satellite, and I hear the Lilly brothers quite often.

Each grade school in Wyoming County had three basketball teams that were organized by weight. All boys that weighed less than 74 pounds were on the "C" team. Those weighing more than 105 pounds were on the "A" team, and the in-betweens were on the "B" team. Each spring all schools participated in a tournament at Pineville, the County seat. Before the tournament, we practiced our skills by playing other schools on an ad hoc basis. Since there was only one school bus to take us home from school, when we played away games we missed the bus.

Our principal, Mr. Ted Clay, a superb person and educator, drove us to the games and back home since our "coach" worked at the mines and practiced with us only after work. He was unavailable for our afternoon games.

I remember playing a game at the McGraws School, formerly the Milam High School where my mom graduated in 1933. The school had no gym, so we played on a concrete pad outdoors with snow flurries falling.

Knighthood

The announcement in the fall 1995 issue of *GOLDENSEAL Magazine*, published by the Division of Culture and History, West Virginia, of the upcoming Golden Horseshoe reunion triggered a memory of a time long ago when I made the trip to Charleston for my own Golden Horseshoe knighting ceremony. For me it was an incredible journey even though it lasted only one day. As a soon-to-be graduate of Maben Grade School, I was already excited with the anticipation of being in the ninth grade and attending high school in the fall. But those feelings were mild compared to what I was to experience on that trip to Charleston that day in 1949.

The Golden Horseshoe Program, in which hundreds of eighth grade students from West Virginia's 55 counties still participate, was already a venerable tradition in my time. The printed brochure for the 2004 ceremony says that the idea goes back as far as 1929, originating with Phil Conley, editor of the old West Virginia Review. Conley promoted "West Virginia Clubs" through his magazine and proposed that the State Department of Education begin competitive testing of eighth grade students as a way to stimulate interest in learning about West Virginia. The superintendent of schools agreed, and the club work and statewide testing soon began.

In my day, the West Virginia Clubs, covering four years beginning with the fifth grade, required students to study the history, geography, and economic development of the State. Eighth graders were tested on this knowledge, as they still are, and the four winners from each county, two boys and two girls, were rewarded with a trip to the State Capitol and were dubbed Knights and Ladies of the Golden Horseshoe. The governor and other high state officials usually attended the ceremony.'

The name of the award goes back in our history to 1716 when Virginia's Governor Alexander Spotswood led an expedition from Williamsburg, then the capital, to the top of the mountains separating Virginia from what is now West Virginia. There the governor gave each member of his party a tiny golden horseshoe in commemoration of the adventurous journey.

My own Golden Horseshoe adventure began very early on a

Saturday morning in May 1949 when my father drove Bill (William Lewis) Sizemore, a neighbor, pal and classmate, and me from Pierpoint across the five miles of narrow, curvy, mountainous State Route 16 to Mullens High School. There we waited for Mrs. Mae Belcher, the Assistant Superintendent of Schools for Wyoming County, to take us to Charleston. Not only was Mrs. Belcher a VIP in my life of barely 14 years, but she lived in a "prefab" house in Saulsville that had been delivered in sections via railroad from some distant place. That was an unimaginable event to reckon with at that stage of my life.

I remember, while we were waiting on Moran Avenue in front of Mullens High School, a paperboy ambled by and stopped to chat for awhile. He wondered what we were about so early in the morning, especially since he had never seen us before. Frank Penn, the paperboy, turned out to be a pleasant and personable guy, and our short visit left a favorable impression on me. Frank, Bill and I soon became classmates at Mullens and remained friends throughout high school.

What happened during our three-hour drive to Charleston left no lasting memories, and my next recollection is of arriving at the capitol building and joining a huge crowd of people. The students from all 55 counties, plus their chaperons and others, created a big group, all of them probably as excited as I was.

As I recall, lunch was served at Charleston's Fruth School. I remember seeing that name etched in an ornamental concrete block located above the door through which we entered. The school building has since been destroyed. Our meal was an unforgettable experience. It was my first time eating spaghetti, and the very first time that I had ever sat at the same table with a black person. I don't recall his name, but he sat directly across from me at the lunch table. I remember him being from Cass, Pocahontas County. I knew that Cass was a few miles from Denmar, on the Greenbrier River, where my Uncle Dewey Cook had just moved to a small dirt farm.

You must realize that at this point in my life, my world consisted of about 100 or so people from a very patriotic small town that had recently sent 37 of their "boys" off to World War II. As I stated earlier, we were what some call a homogeneous society which is to say that all of us were pretty much alike ethnically. Most of the adults thought that FDR sat at the right hand of God, and that John L. Lewis, leader of the mine union, was at the left hand. Up until that time, I had had little experience with Republicans, people of the Jewish or Catholic faiths, or blacks.

Sometime during the day, the Golden Horseshoe group was bussed to Kanawha County Airport as part of a Capital City tour. I vividly remember three fighter planes flying in a tier- formation, circling the airport. That was an awesome sight to a country boy who had never before seen those magnificent machines cutting through the air with such grace. After that I knew deep down that someday I would fly an airplane, and so I did in the early 1960's as a young Army lieutenant. One of the aviators with whom I flew in the West Virginia National Guard was a Major Gus Bortel. Gus was older than I, and, after I told him about that day in 1949, he told me that he believed that he had flown in one of those P-51's on the day of my Charleston visit. He was a lieutenant at the time.

All of the touring was preliminary to the big day's main event. The time had finally arrived for us to meet the State Superintendent of Schools for the knighting ceremony. The culmination of an adventure, which for me had started almost 12 hours earlier, began as someone read the names of the four winners from Barbour, the first county in alphabetical order. The students walked to the front of the auditorium and knelt with bowed heads. This individual ceremony was repeated for winners from each of the 55 counties.

Since I was from Wyoming County and realizing where we fell alphabetically, you will understand that my wait was agonizingly long. At last, the 55th county winners were called. After our names were read, Bill and I, with another winner whose name I don't recall, moved to the front of the auditorium and knelt before W. W. Trent, the State Superintendent of Schools. He placed the sword upon our right shoulders and across our backs and spoke the words: "I knight you in the Order of the Golden Horseshoe." We were given the command to rise, and a 14-caret golden horseshoe pin was pinned to our shirts. Eight years later my baby sister Helen Rebecca was knighted a Lady of the Golden Horseshoe.

Governor Spotswood's original horseshoes carried a Latin motto which translates to "Thus he swears to cross the mountains." The Golden Horseshoe competition instilled some of that mountain climbing, adventuresome spirit in the winners of my day, and I imagine it still does in the winners of today. My world had already grown since the time four years before when we, as fifth graders, had received the small green West Virginia Club books, and it was soon to expand much further. In the ensuing decades, my life's adventures have carried me beyond the hills of home and outside the boundaries of our state. But, I have kept my horseshoe through it all as well as the knowledge of my proud West Virginia heritage.

Outside the Pollin' Place

All elections were held in Maben Grade School. The students were grateful for the holiday, plus it allowed us the opportunity to collect the credit card-sized cards that each candidate passed out. With those cards, we created a deck of cards with which we played a friendly game of poker using wooden matches as the "chips". All of the guys knew what "match poker" was about and how to play.

Election days were a magnet for other exciting events. When the weather cooperated, several folk always gathered in the afternoon on the road just in front of the schoolhouse being careful not to stray onto the school property. Most were there because they had nothing else to do except be the first to know the news about how each candidate was doing in the voting. Voters walking toward the voting booths had to pass workers trying to persuade them to vote for their candidate. Some of the enticements as I recall were pints of moonshine for the voter if he (the "shine" was never offered to the ladies) voted for the right guy for sheriff, justice of the peace or constable. Since all votes were marked on a piece of paper with a pencil, one of the poll workers glanced at the sheet before it was put into the ballot box. After a guy had cast his vote, and, if he voted for the right person, one of the poll workers nonchalantly signaled from one of the school windows. As the voter departed the school grounds, one of the "electioneers" took a pint bottle of moonshine from the trunk of a car and delivered it, rather stealthily, as if two spies were passing state secrets as they passed one another. Strangely everybody obeyed the law of no trespassing as no one ever took the moonshine onto or entered the school grounds on Election Day. Furthermore, it was taboo to have a drink of alcohol before voting! We were law-abiding folk, but there were some local customs that were acceptable and tolerated! A paradoxical process in exercising ones liberties?

We kids knew that as the Election Day progressed into the afternoon, the men would congregate around a fire near the school in order to be the first to hear the election results. As the drinking progressed, the political discussions began to heat up. Of course, in this neck-of-the-hollow, some folk believed that if you could not convince a fellow to agree with your point of view then you were honor bound to settle your differences with your fists. There was always at least a fight or two, which was the reason we boys hung around. We did not want to miss the "fisticuffs". The following paragraphs contain a couple of stories that I can recall happening on two separate Election days.

In a coal camp in the late forties and early fifties, most of the housing was reserved for the white miners and their families. Since there were only a few black people working in the mines, their housing was smaller and built at another location. Even though black and white lived in separate housing, they did the same work inside the mines and drew the same wages, and everybody shopped in the company store. In Maben, the "colored camp" as it was called in those days, was located on a hill above the school with the few houses in total view from the school. In fact, the dirt road came straight down the steep hill and passed in front of the school and onto the bridge located directly in front of the school. Blacks and whites voted at the same polls.

Late one Election Day, several black coal miners were in one of their cars, parked in front of one of the wooden company houses located on the hill in "colored camp". They were drinking the moonshine that each had collected for casting his vote. During their drinking, smoking and socializing, one of the car seats caught fire. The car's owner slowly staggered into one of the houses to fetch a pail of water to douse the fire. While he was gone, his drinking buddies decided to push the car down the hill into Slab Fork Creek to drench the fire. The Creek was about a couple hundred yards down the hill toward the school. Since the "driver" had no car keys, the other two guys pushed the car onto dirt road and started the car rolling down the hill. In those days, the steering and brakes worked whether the engine was running or not. About halfway down the hill, the drunken driver became confused and missed the small road that ran along school property. As a matter of fact, he ran off the entire road and over a ten-foot embankment into the creek sooner than he had anticipated. The car ended up lodging on its nose or grill at about a 60-degree angle as the smoke began to pour out of the open windows. By that time, the flames were visible.

We boys were sitting on the wooden bridge with our feet dangling over the edge. We watched as the events unfolded. The dazed, temporary driver slowly emerged from the burning car and began his staggering trek back up the hill. In the meantime, the car's owner had returned from inside the house with a small pan of water to find his car missing. As he assessed the situation with some vague help from questioning the two drunken guys that had been left standing in front of his house, the car's owner slowly figured out what had just happened. From his viewpoint, he could see his car in the creek, and it was definitely on fire. The car's owner slowly returned to his house and quickly emerged with a single-shot 12-gauge shotgun. As soon as those two guys remaining on the hill saw the shotgun, they started running down the hill toward the guy that had steered the car down the hill. He was puffing and huffing as he staggered up the hill. When the three guys were within 30 or 40 yards of each other, they began to figure out their predicament. Seeing the guy with the shotgun, the "driver" turned and started running back down the hill as fast as any drunken person could run downhill. Finally, the car's owner stopped took dead aim at the three staggering, running guys and pulled the trigger. At that exact moment in time, all three guys running down the steep hill fell on their faces. We boys swore that we could see the buckshot pass just over their heads. After the shot, one of the guys got up with his face bleeding and started to run again. We could not tell whether or not some of the buckshot had hit him. As it turned out, he was not shot. Fortunately for the guys, the single shot 12 gauge had no more shells. Thus ended that's day's excitement.

On another Election Day, a confrontation didn't turn out so well. Late that day, an hour or so before dark and before the polls closed,

I recall watching two guys, both white, fighting on the bridge that crossed Slab Fork Creek in front of the school. This is the same wooden bridge where we observed the burning car episode. Three or four cars were waiting to cross over the bridge after the fighting came to an end. As the fighters grew tired and weary of hitting or getting hit, they began to grapple. As both fell on the bridge's wooden deck, the one ending up on top was sitting on the other guy's chest. He had placed his knees on the bottom guy's arms and had started using his face as a punching bag. Both guys were so drunk on moonshine that neither was coordinated nor had any energy to move quickly in any direction. While the guy on top was resting from thrashing the guy on the bottom, the bottom guy suggested that the one dishing out the punishment should take it easy since in a few minutes he would be on top. Both men finally got to their feet so tired, bloody and so drunk that they could not do anything more. As the guy with the bloodied face staggered around blinded by the blood in his eye and a swollen face, he fell off the bridge. The fall was about 10 feet, and he landed headfirst into the creek bed. He was killed instantly.

Moonshine-the Libation of Mountaineers

Before the 1960s in West Virginia no one could go into any tavern and buy a drink of liquor because it was illegal. Drinking folk had two choices: buy bonded booze from the State Store or moonshine from your local "hollow" bootlegger. Store-bought whiskey was more expensive than moonshine which sold for about two dollars a pint. Also, to purchase bonded whiskey, you had to travel to the State Store in Mullens, which was about five miles down the hollow. Bonded whiskey would not burn, but moonshine produced a beautiful, bluish flame and would power a Model T Ford. Also, moonshine could be "cut" with water which did not affect its taste. In all cases, it took your breath away for several seconds. Taste was less of a priority when you couldn't breathe.

Within our neck of Slab Fork Hollow there was only one supplier of "white lightening", aka moonshine. That was a couple living in a house located halfway between Pierpoint and the Maben Post Office, across the creek from the main road. The house sat on the Virginian Railroad right-of-way near the tracks. The great flood of 2002 destroyed that house which was then vacant.

The guy that ran the bootlegging operations did so openly but quietly, and was generally left alone by the local law. As a matter of fact, at any evening social or music program conducted at the Maben School gym, the sheriff's deputy or a Mullens City cop attended to keep the peace. More often than not, the officer collected the moonshine at the door of the school gym and after the event someone had to take the officer home because he would be too drunk to drive. By the way someone collected all the moonshine that the officer had so all that was lost was what he drank.

The West Virginia State Police were another matter. There were only two troopers stationed at Mullens so they were seen only sparingly. I remember the State Police raiding the bootlegger's house and carrying out gallon jugs (the booze was contained in Coca-Cola syrup glass jugs) of moonshine. They stood on the swinging bridge next to the house and poured the stuff into Slab Fork Creek. The husband was taken to jail while the wife was left home to look after the "youngins ". Once the Police found out that the husband was infected with T.B., they transported him to the Pinecrest Tuberculosis Sanitarium at Beckley. He spent three or four weeks getting rest and gaining weight before being released and sent home. At home he picked up his bootlegging operations as before. While he was absent, his wife kept the business running. When I left home in 1953, that bootlegging operation was in full swing. For the most part, the law left it alone. I suppose it ceased when the bootlegger became disabled with his TB.

We teenagers knew that if you came around the bootleggers' house around three or four o'clock on a Sunday morning that everyone would be in an alcohol-induced sleep. There were bottles with some "shine" left in them scattered around the kitchen. We simply emptied several into one bottle and left. No one ever knew what we had done.

Sure we teenagers tried to drink the "stuff" more than a couple of times, but it burned the inside of our mouths, took our breath away and caused us to lose track of our surroundings. Therefore, my "gang" and I never quite saw the thrill of drinking something that brought tears to your eyes.

For coal miners, moonshine was a weekend and holiday beverage. If a miner or railroader showed up for work with booze on his breath he was fired immediately, no questions asked. Everyone knew that was the case and accepted it without question. Therefore, binge drinking on weekends was the social activity of choice. Since most moonshine sales were by the pint, once the bottle was opened the cap was thrown away and the pint was passed around until it was emptied.

We never knew the location of the still or who supplied the moonshine. The bootlegger did not make it; that much we knew. Also, we teenagers knew that hanging out around a still was dangerous. One could get shot!

We found a recently abandoned still about a mile up one of the hollows from our house. The kettle, copper "worm" or spiral tube used to condense the alcohol steam coming off the boiling mash kettle, was still in place. To boil the fermented mash, bootleggers like to use wood from a dried chestnut tree because it didn't produce smoke when burning. Smoke in the woods was a telltale sign of an illegal operation. We were lucky in that instance because the still was not operating. Those guys would shoot at the crack of a twig!

I once heard of another coal miner that was busted by the sheriff for making moonshine. The county judge sentenced the perpetrator to several months in the county jail. As I recall, it was late summer, and the food crops had to be harvested. The jailed man was responsible for feeding a family of eight people. So in handing out justice, the sheriff let the culprit out during the weekday so he could report to his job, but he had to return to the jail at night. On Saturday mornings, the jailed guy got to go home to tend his crops. He was required to return to the jail on Sunday nights. My quess is that there was a promise to attend church thrown in also. That kind of compassion was considered "fair" justice.

The Chief of Police in Mullens assisted the county sheriff in providing policing duties within our hollow, though he had no jurisdiction. No one argued with that fact since he had a gun and a badge. Plus, if you gave him a hard time or protested in any way, you knew that sooner or later you had to travel to the town of Mullens, which was his domain. Besides, he was my mom's cousin, and we knew that he would look after us. Most folk were law abiding so they welcomed the presence of the Chief. Besides, everybody had known him all their lives.

Rumor had it that one night the Chief stopped a car going the wrong way on a one-way street in the narrow confines of the Mullens streets. He asked the driver where he was from since it was obvious he was lost. The driver said that he was from Chicago. It's said that the Chief rebutted with, "Mister you can't fool me. You got Illinois plates on this car!

Lamentation

Folk born and raised in Appalachia maintain tenacious and lifetime ties to their birthrights. Which is to say, "if you were born here then you are from here." However, if you were *not* born here, even though you have lived at this place for many years, you are accepted as a neighbor, but you are *not* from here!" Their sense of devotion toward one another and their reverence toward their native way of life is steadfast. People and events tied to their locale became the material for embellished tales for future conversation, particularly for impressionable children who heard their stories. After being gone from "home" for more than 50 years, when I go back to Pierpoint the folk that know me treat me as if I still lived there. They will tell me stories about a person that I have not seen for 50 years as if I just saw that individual a day or two before.

"Uncle Bob" Sarver, who lived with his preacher son in our small hamlet, was an old man when I was just seven or eight years old. I always thought that he must have been born about the time General Lee surrendered to General Grant at Appomattox Court House, VA. I don't remember much about Uncle Bob's life, but I do remember the events that took place when he died.

When someone died, the custom at that place and time was for a family member or someone very close to the deceased to build the coffin. With that in mind, the best wide hardwood boards were always collected, seasoned and kept dry in the barn for just that occasion. Likewise, the womenfolk kept pieces of black silk cloth stashed away. It was used to line the inside of a coffin.

Since embalming the deceased person was not considered an option, the body needed to be laid to rest within a day or two, depending upon whether it was summer or winter. That short schedule required that the coffin be built within about twenty-four hours following the death.

One of our neighbors, Arthur Blevins, was also an elderly person and a close friend to Uncle Bob.   Mr. Blevins was a carpenter and cabinetmaker by trade. Both his barn and our house were located on the mountainside of the creek, opposite from the rest of town, on rare bottomland which was created inside of a curve of Slab Fork Creek as it meandered and cut its way through that section of the mountains. Mr. Blevins decided to build the coffin by himself since he had known "Uncle Bob" most of his life, and he was one of his closest friends and probably kin. In such a homogenous small society, we were all related somehow.

For the very same reason that escaped an eight-year old boy at the time, our neighbor needed to vent his emotions and agony from the grief and sorrow that he felt as a result of losing a good friend. Crafting a coffin from rough-hewn boards served to ease his pain as well as fill an obligation to his deceased friend. He was able to make one last contribution to a man for whom he had deep feelings after a long friendship.

Mr. Belvins selected several prime, knotless, hardwood boards that had seasoned into picturesque, alternating wood grains of a dark hue, haphazardly outlining each board as if an artist had painted them. We kids watched his every move hoping to be given some minimum task as each board was planed, for what seemed like hours, with a draw knife. (A drawknife is a woodworker's tool consisting of a blade with handles at each end for use in shaving off wood surfaces. One other use is by a furrier on a horse's hoof to prepare the hoof to receive a shoe. The drawknife is also called a drawshave.) The boards were shaved as smooth as glass.

The coffin was built essentially using six boards. Mr. Blevins began working with the long sideboards, which had to be "bent" to outline the coffin shape that simulates the shape of the human body. Each front and backside took the longest time to shape.   In order to bend the sideboards into the desired shape, vertical grooves were sawed on the board side that faced inside the box, perpendicular to the length.   The grooves were cut to about two-thirds of the board's thickness, and, since the board needed to be bent considerably, the grooves had to be about one inch apart. Once the grooves were sawed, the desired coffin shape was outlined on another board. That board was used as a template gauge. It was used to gauge the degree of bend for the sideboards.

The sideboards were taken outside the barn and laid on a ramp with the grooves on the down side. Burlap fabric was placed upon the boards, taking care to cover the entire board area on the opposite side and over the grooves. Boiling water was slowly poured over the burlap making sure that a steady stream of hot water was gently covering and soaking the boards. That process was continued until the boards were soaked and could be easily bent into the desired coffin shape. Once the side boards were bent into the desired shape, the bottom board, which had been used as a template, was hewed on its edges with a draw knife to exactly fit the inside contour of the curved side boards. Once the bottom board was put into place, several holes were hand drilled through the sideboards into the edge of the bottom board. Wooden dowels were made and driven into the holes to secure the bottom board. The end pieces were cut, hewed and doweled into place. The coffin contained no metal parts!

Next the coffin lid was crafted from a single board which showed the most desirable looking grain pattern. I believe the wood was probably a variety of maple. The lid was hewed to a smooth, satin, glossy appearance with a surface that had been lightly wetted to raise the soft grains so they could be honed with the drawknife. The inside of the lid, as well as the inside of the sideboards, was lined with silk cloth. Since the shape of the lid was exactly the outside dimension of the coffin, it served as a cap for the coffin. Holes were predrilled in the lid for dowel pins that would be placed later at the graveyard after final viewing.

With light from just two oil lamps, Mr. Blevins worked throughout the night never letting up. The work kept him occupied and helped to take his mind of his grief. That was a difficult task for an older man, but his perseverance and staying power, as I recall, were up to the task at hand.

Morning came quickly and Mr. Blevins had completed his task. It was time for the womenfolk, lead by Mrs. Blevins, to line the coffin and make a small pillow for Uncle Bob's head. Several neighborhood men carried the coffin about 75 yards to the back porch of the Blevins' house to make it convenient for the ladies. The womenfolk were not expected to work in the barn. In any case, it took the ladies several hours to place the silk lining inside the coffin. The cloth was cut a little longer than the height of the coffin and as long as the length. The silk was hung wrong side up on the outside and tacked just inside the walls near the top. Then the cloth was flipped inside hanging loosely down the inside wall.

One of the ladies had made a small pillow using feathers from the pillow that Uncle Bob's head was laying on when he died. I don't recall if there was a "crown of feathers" generated inside the pillow, as has occurred on other occasions of death. A "crown of feathers" is a group of feathers tightly woven into a circle of about six inches in diameter similar to a small wreath. This much I do know and that is that they were collected from the pillows that people had their heads upon when they died. The significance of whether one exists or is created when one dies has escaped me. However, there are many folk with "crown of feathers" keepsakes in their cedar chests.

Once the coffin was lined, it was hauled on a sled pulled by a horse to Uncle Bob's son's house. There the empty coffin was carried into the front room and placed upon two hickory cane kitchen chairs lying on their backs with the chair backs toward the wall. Uncle Bob's body was carried from the same bed in which he died and placed into the coffin. His best clothes had been put on him the night before.

The wake, which is conducted for the purpose of making sure that a person is in fact dead, had been performed during the first night after he died. By noon the day after he died, his body was in the coffin and ready for viewing and for the funeral. By late afternoon, the coffin was transported several miles on a dirt road in the bed of an old truck to the base of a mountain on what is called "Bower's Ridge". That is where West Virginia's Twin Falls State Park is now located. The graveyard is located on the hill overlooking the old Bower home place. A preacher delivered a blessing as the coffin was placed on a sled pulled by a team of horses for his final ride. After the coffin was secured to the sled with an old logging chain, the team of horses was directed up the steep hill on an eroded remnant of a dirt road toward the graveyard on Bower's Ridge. Only hardy people could accompany the team up that steep hill.

By dark, the ordeal was over and there was nothing left to do but to go home with a head full of memories from this first funeral for a small boy. As far as I know that may have been the last "free" funeral, not handled by a funeral parlor, and burial that took place in that neck of the woods!

Death and Confusion

One lazy summer afternoon, shortly after World War II, several of us boys were doing what we did most summers, and that was playing in Slab Fork Creek. The creek was adjacent to or near the railroad since, within those steep Appalachian valleys, there was only room for the creek, a road, the railroad and two rows of houses. There were two passenger trains running each day, one eastbound and one westbound. The trains were almost always on time and, along with the angle of the sun, reminded us of the time of day. Also, we enjoyed waving to the passengers. There was never a day that went by in the summertime that we were not aware of the trains. We had been taught to respect the danger because there were several railroad workers that had lost a limb or worse, their lives, in a train incident.

One day while several of us boys were swimming at one of our favorite sites, the "Ben Byrd" hole, we were anticipating the eastbound passenger train so we could wave to the passengers. Instead we heard the train's brakes, which made a loud, eerie, screeching noise just before the engine passed our site. That quickly got our attention since we knew it took the train several hundred feet to come to a complete stop. Every boy in the creek quickly looked toward the noise to see what was happening to cause the train to make a "panic" stop. In our young lives, we had never heard the passenger train brakes applied in that manner. To our horror, we saw the train hit a man.

We were familiar with that man who lived with and was being cared for by his brother's family. He had returned from the war that left him in a condition that we kids called "loco", but we were told the medical or military diagnosis for his predicament was called "shell-shocked". That guy wandered around town totally in his own world. He never bothered a soul, and being a small town full of caring people, everyone was sympathetic to his condition. If he appeared lost or confused, someone led him home.

The cowcatcher, which serves as the front bumper of the steam engine and is positioned a few inches above the top of the tracks, hit his legs causing his body to make a backward somersault. He landed in a horizontal position on his back on the railroad berm of cinders and crushed rock next to the crossties. The entire train continued to slide along the tracks for several hundred yards before coming to a complete stop.

We ran up the grade from the creek and continued at a full pace toward the accident. We were the first ones to arrive to attend to the injured man. Our first impression upon arriving at the site was that he was knocked out because there was no blood or other visible signs of injury. Since I arrived on the scene a little ahead of the others, my first instinct was to put my hand behind his head and lift it up to see if he was still conscious. I was hoping to render some aide to him. As I slipped my hand behind his head and started to lift his head upright, my entire hand went into the back of his open skull. Stunned, I quickly dropped his head onto the cinders since I knew he was dead. Afterwards we noticed parts of his brains scattered on the tracks.

Hearing the sounds of that train braking, most of the townsfolk, particularly our parents, also ran toward the railroad noise with thoughts that one of us kids had been run over by the train. I remember my mom hurried up to me. She wasn't sure whether to hit me or hug me, so she gave me a great big hug. Finally, someone brought a sheet and covered the body as the train continued on its way. As other people arrived, I left the accident scene and started toward the town proper where the dead soldier's brother lived.

When the dead soldier's brother was told that he had died instantly after being hit by a train, his first words were "I don't have the money to bury him". Since that day, I have put money way down on my list of what's important to me. After 50 years' memory of this incident, I still don't understand how that can be a person's first thought when learning that his brother has just loss his life.

Appalachian Weekend
Huntin' Parties

Omeda Cook Halsey (author's mom) with
groundhogs.
Youngest daughter, Helen, on her right
circa 1949

Chapter 5
Appalachian Weekend Huntin' Parties

*"What David loved about his childhood was the freedom. Living in the
mountains gave him a lot of creative things to do and plenty of spaces to do them in. There
were no restrictions; they could wander for hours."* Jason David Halsey 1989

There was a place that we loved to visit. It was a small dirt farm
located about a mile off the "hardtop" road, nestled on a small parcel of
level land at the head of a hollow that was carved out by two creeks that
merged to form the main creek. That creek flowed out of the hollow.
There perched on a small hill overlooking the paved road was the Pine
Grove Church and cemetery near a hamlet with a post office called
Ravencliff. The day-to-day chores had not changed there since it was
settled years before. That farm belonged to my Uncle Evert and Aunt
Pearl Acord, mom's older sister, and their family. My cousins, five boys
and three girls, grew into adulthood at that place. By the time I was old
enough to visit and stay overnight, the oldest cousin, Lee, had traveled to
Utah to work with the Conservation Job Corps, called the CCC. After
that he joined the Navy and was killed in the south Atlantic just before
WWII started. He was with a small crew of sailors assigned to help man
a Merchant Marine ship. That particular ship's mission was to evacuate
missionaries from North Africa. A German U-boat sank the merchant
marine ship and evidently shot some of the survivors on a raft, including
Lee. Another cousin, "Sister", who's given name was Lottie, had also
left the home hollow to start her own family in Ravencliff, a mile or two
from the Pine Grove Church.

On that small farm, the family raised and canned more than
enough food to support all of them. The home place featured a small,
weather beaten, wood-framed house, with no electricity or indoor
plumbing. Nearby in one of the small hollows was a small barn that was
home to a milk cow and an old horse named "Old Dan". Old Dan was
nearly blind, but he could work a few hours a day. His human handlers
were his eyes; if he was left on his own, he would walk into a tree or
other object. Near the hog pen, there was a corncrib that attracted a
colony of chipmunks that conveniently made their burrows nearby. The
cellar, used for keeping food cool and as a place to store canned goods,
was located just to the left of the house. The drinking and cooking water
came from a nearby spring. The left hollow was always protected from
farm animals and anything else that could contaminate the water supply.
The barn and hog pen were located to the right of the house.

The only electric device present in the house was a radio
powered by a battery that was bigger than the radio itself. When I first
visited, I learned that we were allowed to turn on the radio only on
Saturday nights to listen to the Grand Old Opry. Saving the battery was

important since there was no way to recharge it, and it was expensive to replace. One time when it became weak, someone placed the battery on the warm cook stove for rejuvenation. I don't recall if the warmth of the stove did any good or not, but in later years I realized that the battery could have easily exploded. The radio antenna was a wire, about 10-15 feet long with the insulation stripped off, strung between the limbs of two large oak trees that overshadowed the house. The necks from two broken Coke bottles were used to insulate the antenna. Once the antenna was moved around for the best reception, it was secured in place. On special occasions, that orientation allowed us to hear, without too many fading pulses or static, the broadcast from several clear channel radio stations including WSM's Grand Old Opry from Nashville.

From our house, whenever we planned to visit our cousins, it was simply referred to as "going over to Uncle Evert's or Aunt Pearl's". Uncle Evert worked on the night shift at a coal mining operation located at Glen Rogers. Every evening after supper, he walked the mile to the mouth of the hollow dressed in his work clothes and carrying a metal lunch bucket. He met his carpool at the Pine Grove Church. Later, when he bought a Chevy pickup, he drove himself. Working at night and farming during the daytime with a large family that did their chores provided a good life as no necessities were lacking. All the children graduated from Glen Rogers High School. A couple of the boys played high school football in addition to keeping up with their farm chores. As a matter of fact, I believe Jack, one of the older brothers, played an extra year using his younger brother Dale's name.

One of the farm pets was a groundhog. It had been hand-raised from a baby. Its name was Billie, and it had dug a den under the house. Billie would stand on his/her (no one ever knew its gender) hind legs and whistle in response to a human's whistle. You could pet and feed him from your hand, but we all knew that he was a wild animal and that sooner or later he would react accordingly. Several times Billie was caught taking a sheet from the clothesline. He tried to pull the sheet into his den. When he did something bad, he was put into his screened-box home as punishment for a day or two. One time Billie got so sick that everyone thought that he was going to die. He was in his box lying completely lifeless. Some sulfur drug, the wonder drug of that era, was found in the house, and someone decided to cram it into Billie's mouth. Low and behold, he perked up in a day or so and was acting normal again. One time while the entire family was away for a day, Billie disappeared, and one of the neighbors was suspected of having eaten Billie for supper.

Almost every dirt farmer in Appalachia nurtured several stands (hives) of honeybees. Caring for the bees did not take much effort or resources, but it did require certain care and seasonal maintenance activities. For example, the type and taste of honey that the bees produced depended upon what flowers were blooming at the time. Different flower blooms produce honey that has a distinct taste and texture as well as color.

Every spring the worker bees[4] swarmed because almost every hive produced extra queens. In the bee hierarchy, only one queen per hive is allowed. The queens will fight until one is dead unless the new queen leaves the hive. Upon departure, she will take a good portion of the worker bees with her to form a colony elsewhere, generally in a hollow tree in the forest. Sometimes every worker bee in the hive will follow the new queen. That is called swarming.

Whenever honeybees swarmed, it got real noisy, not from the buzz of the bees but from the people beating a dishpan with a wooden spoon or rattling a pot with a metal spoon inside. Water from large pails was flung toward the bee swarm in hopes of hitting the new queen and knocking her to the ground. If she was killed or captured the worker bees returned to the original hive. Everyone was desperate to save the bees and killing the new queen was the only way to accomplish that.

Sometimes the bees settled on the limb of a nearby peach tree. Why the swarming bees are attracted to the peach tree remains a mystery to me. The peach tree must give off some kind of aroma that the bees like. On more than one occasion, I helped my uncle Mace, who was married to my dad's sister Beatrice, take a gallon or so of bees from a nearby peach tree and place them into a hive. The queen was easy to spot since they are longer, bigger and lighter in color. We just plucked her up, since queens have no stinger and placed her in the new hive. All the worker bees came to their new home like royal subjects. That is rare since most of the swarms continue to fly to destinations unknown.

When a hunting trip provided us the opportunity to hunt for "wild" bees to replenish our bee population, we took advantage of the situation. In the mountains, small streams that remain moist in the dry season meander toward the bottomland and, on the way, leave small sandbars on the flat portions along the streambed. The moist sand presented an ideal place for the bees to collect moisture. Our hunting parties looked for bees at those sandbars as we trekked up the hollow toward our hunting grounds.

When we found a bee taking on moisture, which we called "watering", we took a long stem of broom sage straw, dabbed it in silver paint that we carried in an old medicine vile, and put a drop on the bee's rear end. That made it easier to spot the bee when it was flying toward its colony. The sunlight reflected from the paint. We would systematically track several bees to mark the direction of flight until we were satisfied that

---

[4] A hive contains three kinds of bees: (1) queen; (2) worker; and (3) drones or males. The drones mate with the queen. Afterwards the worker bees kill them and their bodies are deposited on the ground outside the hive. Only the worker bees produce honey, wax and support the queen.

we had the approximate bearing toward what became "the bee tree". Once the bees lifted up above the treetops, they flew straight toward their "bee tree" home. We would continue through the trees and over the mountains taking great pains to periodically stop and listen, since a large population of bees makes a lot of buzzing noise.

Once we had located and marked a bee colony on a hunting trip, we would return a couple of weeks later hoping to find that the bees had taken up residence in a hollow tree. The colony was easy to spot because wax covered their entrance, which was a large hole created by a rotting knot. Harvesting honey from a beehive is called "robbing the hive". The only way to harvest a "stand" of bees was to cut down the tree. So that's what we would do! As a tree hit the ground, the trunk would split open along its entire length spewing honeybees and possibly several years of honey accumulation. One time a split tree three feet in diameter landed a few feet above the ground, resting upon its broken limbs. Once bees were disturbed by that much violence, they became mean, stinging everything they touched. So a head veil and gloves were always necessary protection for any individual trying to find a queen. If we found the queen, we placed her in the beehive that we brought with us, and the worker bees that were swarming around trying to protect her would follow. That time we could not find her. We did not know her fate after the tree had fallen. We collected and ate some of the honey from the fallen tree and placed some of it inside the beehive as bait. If the bees took up residence in the hive, we could retrieve the hive after dark when they were all home for the night.

In that particular instance, the hive was placed upon the broken tree at a strategic location, and my cousins and I departed for home. Three or four days later, we returned to collect our new bees. When we arrived at the site, we found nary a bee buzzing around. We arrived before dusk so we could make sure we had bees. It was hard to accept that, after all that effort, we could not find a single bee. We wondered what could have happened to the hundreds of bees that were swarming around when we had left our beehive.

As I approached the beehive, which was resting upon the fallen tree, I did so from the opposite side of the split trunk. I jumped forward onto the fallen tree, landing on the pit of my stomach so I could lean my head over the top to see inside the split-hollow tree. It seemed safe enough since there were apparently no bees present. As I bent over the fallen tree with my head hanging upside down, I looked down the inside of the tree to the extreme right and then turned my head toward the left, but as I turned to the exact center I froze. About two or three inches from my nose, stretched long ways inside the tree was the largest copperhead that I had ever seen! It apparently had about a gallon of bees in its long stomach. Fortunately, it was too full to care about me and in no position to strike. I quickly pushed myself backward with a powerful arm thrust, scared to death.

Most of the meat for the table was harvested from hunting excursions generally taken on the weekends. Butchering several hogs in the fall supplemented the wild meat plus it added lard, liver, sausage, bacon, pork chops and ham to the breakfast menus.

About everything that I know about hunting was gleaned from my experiences with four of my first cousins on my mother's side. They were Buddy and Glen Cook and Jack and Freeman Acord, Uncle Evert's sons. They were a few years older than my brother Richard and me, yet they treated us as peers. When we were around those guys, whether it was on the farm or in the woods, we got to take part in most of the activities. They were the big brothers that I didn't have. They shepherded all of us with the attitude and toleration of a big brother as we learned how to be successful hunters. Their brotherly love and patience never wavered. When things were going wrong, I can still hear Glen uttering, in his redheaded, high tenor voice, the closest he ever came to expressing frustration. He would say **"landsakes"**!

I vividly remember multiple hunting trips to gather meat. They began on a Friday afternoon and lasted until late Sunday night. We sometimes spent time collecting ginseng root. At that time, dried ginseng fetched about $10 per pound at the market, so it was worth harvesting. I loved to chew the root, so I was not allowed to carry any that had been dug because I chewed up the profit.

Having been taught how to hunt by cousins, Glen and Buddy, I was always ready to do my share with confidence. Uncle Evert and his gang of sons, along with my brother, Richard, and me, would work our way up one of the small creek branches from the home place to start our hunting journey. We made our way deeper into the mountains. In that part of the mountains, the only critters left to hunt were groundhogs, squirrels, raccoons, and occasionally grouse. Wild game had been hunted out close to home so any successful hunting had to be done several miles into the mountains. While on those trips, we also were on the lookout for bees.

Darkness always seemed to come upon us quickly, as we were often preoccupied with the bees. We walked as deep into the woods as necessary until it was time to find a campsite. One time in particular, Uncle Evert, cousins Jack, Freeman, and their younger brothers Dale and Tracy, my brother, Richard, and I found a level spot near an old abandoned pioneer home place that had what used to be the house near a grassy, shady spot close to a small creek. It was late evening of what turned out to be a long day. Everyone was tired from spending time locating the bee tree, from walking several miles in the mountains, and from digging a groundhog from his hole.

To keep the groundhog "fresh", it had been gutted earlier in the day and stuck under a rock in the cool water of a nearby stream. Later that evening, we skinned the "hog" and started the cooking process. To make the critter edible, the carcass had to be cooked all night in boiling water, which meant that somebody had to keep the fire burning.

Typical fare for Friday night supper was pork 'n beans and cornbread with coffee. The cornbread was baked before we left home, wrapped in a dishtowel, and lasted for a weekend of hunting. Corn for the bread meal was raised on the farm, and, after it had dried in the corncrib, it was taken to a local stone grinding mill and ground for a fee that was a share of the ground meal. The first time in my young life that I can remember drinking coffee was on one of those hunting trips. Breakfast sometimes consisted of groundhog cut into small pieces and fried in lard . It was served with pork 'n beans and cornbread.

I remember once, during the first evening at a campsite, that one of my older cousins (no names please) was "milking" one of our best hunting bitches into his coffee cup! She had just given birth to several pups. Since we had more than enough dogs, the pups had to be destroyed. They were placed in a burlap bag with a large rock and thrown into the deep end of the creek. It was a cruel deed but necessary since we had no way to neuter the dogs. About once or twice a day, it was necessary for someone to "milk" the bitch, otherwise her teats would be so full of milk that they became painful to the dog and hung down causing her to refuse to hunt. She was our best dog, so we pampered her. Since he liked cream in his coffee and that was the only milk available, he decided to use it. I have always drunk my coffee black!

One night I recall that everyone had found a comfortable place close to the fire for warmth since we had brought no blankets. I remember seeing a piece of tin roof lying nearby. I decided to lie upon it to sleep instead of getting dirty from sleeping on the ground. Once darkness arrived, the only light that we had came from the fire, so we stayed put. Critters like timber rattlesnakes and bobcats were frequently on the prowl at night. All during that particular night, I could never get comfortable. I tossed, rolled and tumbled as if I was lying on rollers. The next morning after daybreak, I decided to pick up the piece of tin to find out what was under it that had caused me to lose a good night's sleep. As I flipped it over, a large black snake, slightly irritated from being trapped and rolled all night under the tin, took off for its freedom in the bushes!

After breakfast we would clean up the campsite, douse the fire, and continue the hunt. Both dogs, the bitch and the male, were lop-eared hounds. As I recall, the male was a blue tick named "Old Sam", and the bitch was a black and tan called "Old Girtie". The hunting on those outings always included a search for fresh meat for our breakfasts and suppers. Groundhog always tasted real good with pork 'n beans and fried corn pone (fried cornbread). After we turned the dogs loose, their instinct was to hunt so we let them lead us through laurel thickets up the mountain in search of groundhog, sometimes called a woodchuck or whistle pig.

Often we went up a draw that had small pools of water mixed with gravel. There were thick patches of nettle weed on both sides as we trekked along. In late summer, the nettle weed had matured making the leaves a little tougher and the sting sharper. It grows about two feet high with large leaves that irritate the skin. There were clearings that were the result of past forest fires, and we were always hopeful that we would come upon one so we could avoid the nettle weed. Old Sam was always in the lead because he was more aggressive, but we trusted Girtie more because she was more reliable. Both dogs would follow their noses as they swept back and forth as if intoxicated. Their noses remained only a fraction of an inch above the ground as they ran at three-quarters speed trying to pick up the scent of a critter. Usually, Old Sam would break away indicating his find with a bark. We knew that he had made contact with a familiar scent. As the pace picked up, and Sam's gate had straightened, he would "yelp". It sounded as if he had his tail caught in a vise. That indicated to us that the groundhog's scent was strong, and Sam's instincts were telling him that the critter was nearby. When threatened, a groundhog would run toward one of its many holes.

Normally, when a whistle pig is chased, it will immediately dive into its hole, make a complete turn and then poke his head back out to observe or assess the situation. I recall a game that we used to play where we attempted to sneak up on a "pig" that was basking in the sunshine, which they apparently like to do when not feeding on the vegetation. Before we played that game with the groundhog, we had to reconnoiter the area to determine where the den was located in relation to the sunning log or rock. Also, we equipped ourselves with a club. For example, an ax handle made of hickory was an ideal club. Then we tried to sneak up on the pig. When he discovered our presence, he made a beeline for his den. Our reaction time had to be quick because groundhogs were so fast that we would not have a chance of hitting one. As we approached to about ten feet from the opening of the den, we had to dive toward it with the ax handle cocked and ready to strike. As we landed on our bellies, we had to swing the ax handle toward the den opening hoping that our timing was the same as his. We tried this trick many times with absolutely no success.

When the dog's bark sounded muffled, it meant they had their head in a groundhog's hole. "Holed", Uncle Evert would holler. "Must be a groundhog." We would continue our climb up the mountainside until we finally reached the location of the dogs. Both dogs would be side by side digging frantically. Everyone knew that we had to quickly begin the digging because the pig was busy blocking the hole to protect itself in a futile attempt for isolation. Someone would cut a long twig from a nearby maple tree. The little end of the twig was cut at a fork being careful to leave a "y" on the end. The small end of the twig was inserted into the hole in a probing fashion as the hole consumed most of the twig. As soon as it felt like the twig hit something, it was gently twisted and slowly withdrawn from the hole. The end was then checked for hair. That evidence confirmed that the groundhog was in fact inside the den! Also, the probing indicated in which direction the hole ran so we knew in which direction to dig. We didn't dig out the entire hole. We dug a series of trenches that intercepted the passageway.

A groundhog normally digs a den with more than one opening and a passageway depth of about three or four feet below the surface, just enough to put it below the winter frost line. We would dig two intercepting trenches with our mattock in an effort to see the groundhog that was always poised, ready to defend his abode against all odds and any eventuality.

Uncle Evert had a thick leather belt with an oversized wire-type brass buckle on one end. He would take the belt from his pants and hook the outside end of the buckle onto the fork of the little end of the maple branch. With the twig holding the belts buckle, it was presented to the groundhog's face. As expected, the groundhog would plant his large front teeth over the belt buckle. Once a groundhog sets his bite, he will not turn lose. With the pig's large teeth overlapping the buckle with a bite of great determination, he was slowly pulled out of his den exposing him to our hounds! Old Sam and old Girtie were beside themselves because they knew the fight would soon begin once the groundhog was exposed.

Sam was the most aggressive, and he had to be kept out of the den area where he could get hit with a mattock. When the groundhog was exposed, Sam was turned loose. That big dog took about two steps to cover ten meters. Contact was made as one beast lunged toward the other. That time the dog won as his mouth was large enough to grab the belt buckle as well as the groundhog's head and shoulders. Nothing could be heard over the sound of bones cracking. End of hunt! We gutted that pig and placed it under a rock in the cool creek and continued our hunt. We picked up the critter on our way back to the campsite.

Boys Will Be Boys - Games, Pranks and Dares

David & cousin, Margie Cox

Chapter 6
Boys Will Be Boys – Games, Pranks and Dares

"The Early Years-For fun David and his brothers turned over outhouses, dodged the bullets that the outhouse owners shot at them, hopped trains, went into abandoned coal mines, took big lumps of coal and sold them, and swam in creeks." Jason David Halsey 1989

I cannot ever remember having a day when there was not something interesting to do such as fishing, hunting, hillside farming and locally created games like "tag" and what we called "duck-on-a-rock" and marble games with such unusual names like "fatty", "ring" and "rolly hole".

Duck-on-a-rock was a hide-and-seek type game played in darkness with a different twist. The required equipment consisted of a tin can, a stick and a flat rock. The can was placed upon the rock, and, after it was struck with the stick by one of the other players, whoever had been chosen to be "it" retrieved the can and placed it back on the rock. The "it" person had to count to 25 before he could begin searching for the other players who were hiding. Once the "it" person found someone, he had to race back to touch the can before that player. To be successful, the "it" person had to establish a search pattern by spiraling out from the can and rock. He had to keep the can in view at all times, in spite of the darkness; otherwise he could never win. The "it" player had to win the race to the can so that the losing player became the "it" person.

Tag was only played by the hearty who could run, up, down, and sometimes over the surrounding mountains. A game normally lasted all day and generally involved six to eight boys. Since the steep mountains surrounded us, this huge amphitheater-like setting provided a unique place in which to play a game of tag. As in the prior game, somebody had to be "it". The rest of us ran into the wooded mountainsides for a day of pursuit and deception. The ultimate object of that game was to have the "it" person looking for you on one mountainside while you were diagonally across town on another mountain, a mile or so away. Several of us boys could get the attention of the "it" person by whistling. Some learned early how to whistle by putting two fingers in one's mouth and blowing. I never learned to whistle, but I did learn to make a sound like an owl by clasping my coupled hands a certain way on my mouth and blowing air at a certain pressure. Both methods created sounds that could be heard a mile or so away. Once recognition was established, the "it" person knew that he was not going to catch anyone that day. Of course, the next day was spent telling "war" stories about our cunning and expert deception and how we did not get "tagged". Each story was inflated on every point as to how each got away and how close our encounters were during the game.

Marbles games were dad's favorite pastime so by the time we were eight or nine, he had taught us how to shoot so well that we could out play most adults. Each player, over time and with experience, accumulated the tool of the trade called a "steelie" which served as a taw. The steelie was a steel ball about a quarter inch in diameter taken from the ball bearings in mining machinery. It had to weigh more than the glass marbles, be comfortable in one's hand and easy to shoot with the thumb. Steelies were easy to find around a mining operation. Each shooter crafted a special piece of leather to serve as a pad to protect the knuckles of the shooting hand from touching the ground while shooting. Also, each person had a bag or sack for marble storage.

The object of the most often played game called "ring" was to shoot the steelie from the outer boundary denoted by a line scribed on the ground outlining a 10-foot ring. The goal was to strike the marbles that were anted up and placed in a bunch near the ring's center. The taw was shot by resting it snuggly between the forefinger and thumb and propelling it with the thumb with enough force to knock a marble(s) outside the ring while attempting to get the taw to "stick" or come to rest inside the ring. If those two things happened, then that player got another turn from the spot where his taw came to rest inside the ring. A player continued trying to knock the marbles outside the ring boundary until he missed, didn't knock a marble outside the ring, or his taw left the ring and/or no marbles were left to shoot. Any marble knocked outside the ring belonged to the shooter.

The skills developed by each marble shooter were many and precise. Winning consistently placed a player above the rest. His prestige and respect were great, at least at the company store's nightly forums. The best shooters were our local "heroes", which meant that no one intentionally invited him into a marble game. Enhanced recollections of the shooting feats were the subject of many winter conversations in the evening while gathered around the pot-bellied stove at the company store. Dad was a marble-shooting champion. He seldom, if ever, lost a match and thus had a hard time convincing others to allow him to participate. I remember when he had collected many Mason quart jars full of marbles of all colors.

Years later, after I had left home, my youngest sister, Helen, won the Wyoming County, WV, marble championship. Go girl! My brother and I were also excellent marble shooters. Maybe the skills were passed on to our generation genetically?

"Rolly hole" was a marble game in which six to eight holes were positioned on flat ground about ten feet apart in a zigzag pattern. The holes were about the size of a large coffee cup, dug without a berm so the top was flush with the ground. Each player agreed to "put up" or ante up a certain number of marbles to start the game. Each shooter started at a line drawn on the ground, located about ten feet or so from the first hole. The object of the game was to shoot, in turns, your marble or "taw" into each hole in succession. For each player's turn, he attempted to shoot his marble into the correct hole. If successful, then he got to shoot again. If a player hit another player's "taw", he had to go back to the beginning and start over when it was his turn. After a player had entered all the holes in succession, he was designated what we called a "stinger". Whenever the stinger's turn came about, he could shoot at the marbles of the other players. If a "stinger" hit your marble or "taw", you were out of that game. The game continued until someone had "stung" everyone else's taw. The winner collected all the marbles put up for that game.

The marble game of "fatty" was a winner-take-all game. A player could lose after taking only one shot. Each player anted up an agreed number of marbles that were placed inside a small triangle drawn on the ground. The number of marbles anted up dictated the size of the triangle. Each shooter, in turn, started at a line about 10 feet from the "fatty" triangle. The object was to knock the marbles out of the fatty triangle with your "taw". Whenever you did, those marbles belonged to you until another shooter hit your "taw" during his turn to shoot. He had a choice of shooting at the marbles in the triangle or at your "taw" realizing that if he missed your taw, he was in danger of having you take a shot at him. If he hit your marble, he collected what marbles you had knocked from the triangle, and you were out of the game. The last guy standing won all the marbles that were anted up.

As the fall season slowly drifted into winter, the amount of daylight decreased by a minute or two each day as the sun's angle became lower in the sky. The reality that the nights were getting longer than the days always set in around the time fall colors made their appearance in October. Eventually, there was almost no daylight left for us as we returned home via a school bus. Our daily routines changed with the seasons. In winter our activities shifted to the gatherings that took place around the potbellied stove at Herb Morgan's store. Herb was dad's first cousin. There we listened to the adults discuss the major events of the day. Sometimes we were allowed to join in the discussions. Almost every evening after school, when the chores were done and supper was over, we teenage boys (girls were not allowed out after dark) would slowly mosey over to Herb's to absorb the daily edition of those "round table" discussions.

Most of the men folk had known each other most of their lives. Yet it seemed that the same subjects could be "discussed" by the same people almost every night, and each night produced different conclusions. Whatever triggered those friendly arguments among the local participants was a mystery to me. That was the fun part of it all. From one night to the next night, some guys changed their arguments. My guess is they discussed it over with their wives and got their minds changed. Also, someone that they respected may have taken the opposite side, so the next night they sided with that person. That was the environment in which I learned to take any side of any argument and debate that side regardless of my views. That was an incentive for learning more about a particular subject. It also made some people mad, those who joined your side and found out the next night that you had switched sides! That was how I unintentionally learned how to "brainstorm" a subject which is a technique that served me very well later in life.

As Halloween approached, "potbellied stove" conversations eventually got around to the adults questioning us teenage boys about what destructive escapades, "trick or treat", that we were about to impose upon the citizens of Pierpoint. They wanted to know what we had in mind for property such as outhouses or fodder shocks. They anticipated that pranks were going to take precedent over games. There was always a sort of banter between the different generations as to whose feats were the more spectacular or destructive, depending upon your point of view. Of course, each tale grew in stature each time it was repeated. We all had heard the tall tales before and remembered how facts became more fictional as each year passed.

I'm not proud of what we did, but since it happened, maybe writing this story will serve the purpose of clearing my conscience, although it's about 50 years late. An apology to the Pierpoint folk would probably be more appropriate!

Most of the older generation, who were gathered around the stove chewing tobacco and/or smoking, could recollect the times when they too took their turns at being "hoodlums" on Halloween night. It appeared to us teenage boys that for the most part this type of confined mischief was expected of us as well as accepted, sort of, by the older men. Seldom did any resident make any public comments about what we boys were going to be forbidden to do on Halloween. No one wanted to challenge the egos of a group of teenage boys. Of course, we were aware of the pranks that were "permissible". They had to be somewhat mild, fall into the traditional "outhouse" and/or fodder shock mold, with a result of little or no property destruction, and definitely involve no bodily harm. The outhouses and fodder shocks were not classified as property, at least not on Halloween night.

During one summer, we stashed several sticks of TNT and electrical firing caps with some electrical wire, called shooting wire, for a Halloween midnight fireworks celebration. We wanted to do something distinctly different so that our generation would be remembered as the ones that pulled off this great feat. Sound familiar? All we needed to find before the end of October was a firing battery, and so we did.

I remember digging out the explosives that we had buried a few months before and finding that the sticks of dynamite appeared to be wet. At the time, we didn't know that the nitroglycerin would separate and seep out over a short period of time. In routine storage, the TNT sticks were normally used every few weeks to prevent seepage. In any case, we had a situation that could have been dangerous if there had been enough nitro to cause an explosion. The stuff is very unstable. Maybe that was why we always heard that TNT stood for "taint nothin' to it". In any case, unbeknownst to us, our guardian angels were working overtime as they looked over our shoulders while we prepared our blast.

We selected the rock cliff high above and overlooking the town on the east side since it would be easier to get to from the road that went up Pierpoint Mountain. In our younger years, we had played Cowboys and Indians in and around those rock formations during the daylight, but I had never been up there when it was dark, so it felt really strange. Also, there was a cave where we hid our supplies on the other side of the same rock formation. I had planned to use the cave as a shelter from the blast. I'm not sure where the other guys hid during the blast. I recall that we had less than 10 sticks of TNT and about three electrical firing caps. When we arrived on top of the mountain in the dark of night, we soon discovered that there was only about 100 feet of shooting wire. We found a spot along the length of wire that provided the shooter with some protection from the blast. It was under a large rock that had been lifted up a couple of feet by the trunk of a huge oak tree as it grew from the rock formation. That rock was about as big as a small car and was positioned so that the force from the blast should not cause it to fall on whoever put the wires to the battery terminals to set off the TNT. In fact, the rock was imbedded about a foot into the tree, where, over many years, the tree tried to engulf the rock. So it was very stable.

Everything appeared to be set, and without a timepiece we guessed that midnight, the bewitching hour, was upon us. I can still remember how dark the sleepy little town of Pierpoint appeared with its 100 plus inhabitants all fast asleep. Almost every light was off, but they got a wake up call unlike any they had ever witnessed before.

In any case, it was time to choose who was going to touch the wires to the old battery. Since we were all scared but would not admit it, we decided that at least two people were needed to insure that the TNT was set off. Somehow I and a buddy were selected. I absolutely don't remember who the other guy was. I was really scared. I do remember climbing in between the rock and tree into a crevice filled with wet, decaying leaves from years gone by. We had no thoughts of snakes or other creepy critters being in those crevices. The adrenaline rush caused by the anticipation of the impending blast dominated our minds. My thoughts were to get on with it, so in spite of both of us shaking like leaves in a windstorm, we finally touched the wire to the battery. We didn't realize how close we really were to the blast since, in the dark, distances seem farther apart than they really are.

The blast caused rocks to fly through the trees like bullets, making whistling sounds that were gone in a flash. The rock formation on top of the mountain was solid and carried the vibrations from the blast to our location without any apparent dampening effect. We could not separate the effects caused by the air pressure changes and the rock shaking because we felt the entire effect from the blast. We sat cramped in the crevice for a long time before we decided that we had indeed survived that totally senseless act that definitely woke up a sleepy town. By the time we crawled out of the rocks, every light in town had come on.

War stories describing our Halloween exploits abounded for many weeks afterwards, yet not one of us owned up to being a participant. As far as I know, this is the first time anyone has made an effort to talk about the blast of 1950. I suppose we kept secrets better than the military.

A favorite vandalistic exploit on Halloween involved turning over outhouses and knocking over several fodder shocks. What used to be the one-room schoolhouse, that I attended from first through third grades, rested about halfway up the hill toward the graveyard north of town. By 1950, the old school had become a residence with the two outhouses, one for boys and one for girls, still in use. One Halloween the guy living there at the time had been bragging for sometime that he was going to stay up all night to guard his outhouses and that no kid was going to turn them over. Each outhouse sat upon a concrete holding tank that was pumped out regularly by guys we called "honey dippers". We knew that those toilets would be difficult to turn over in the daylight hours much less in the pitch black of nighttime. They were heavy, built solid, and the boards had not rotted at the base as usually happened to most outhouses.

Sure enough the guy sat on his back porch with two electric lights burning and a 22-caliber rifle lying across his lap. We knew that our only chance to turn over the johns was to surround them with a rope and pull downhill. Well, downhill was in the direction of the guy's porch. First we had to find some rope. We thought maybe we would take somebody's clothesline.

Just to the left and slightly up the hill from that house was an old abandoned coal mine that was worked during the so-called "wagon" mining operational days of the depression years in the early 1930s. In those mines, miners dug coal by hand and pushed it outside in a rail car or makeshift wheelbarrow and dumped the coal into horse drawn wagons that were positioned under a wooden bin with a shoot to direct the coal into the wagons. Thus, the label "wagon mines" was applied to that type of mining.

Later, before electric or gasoline motors powered mining equipment, small ponies were used to pull the loaded coal cars out of the mines. The ponies were worked all day, and we kids would try to ride them at night. The ponies were so short that we couldn't sit on their backs without dragging our feet on the ground.

The opening of an old wagon mine was called a "drift mouth". That particular old mine opening was filled with leaves, twigs and limbs from the hickory forest that covered the eastern slopes and was almost completely covered over from years of erosion and banks sluffing into the mouth. We surmised that place would give us adequate protection if the guy with the rifle really did decide to take a shot at us. Also, that was an ideal place from which to pull on the rope that we anticipated putting around the outhouses. But, first we had to crawl to the outhouses and attach the rope. That was our dilemma.

After a few hours of darkness, the man was still guarding his outhouses. Occasionally, he nodded off as if he was about to fall asleep. We did not know if he was faking the nods or was really getting sleepy. Since we assumed that he had worked in the coal mine that day, we thought that he was probably tired. So we waited patiently for him to fall sound asleep while sitting upright in his old, cane, hickory-frame kitchen chair.

As we crawled through the hickory timber from the drift mouth of the abandoned mine, we made a lot of noise in the dry leaves. Once we were about 20 or so feet from the old mine shaft, he woke up. From his position, the porch light prevented him from seeing any distance into the dark, but he could hear us as we crawled along. Frustrated, he fired a shot through the trees in our general direction. I can still remember the sound of that small 22 bullet as it whizzed through the bushes above our heads. One of our guys who remained safely hunkered down in the abandoned mine shaft, yelled, "shoot again you son-of-a-bitch, you missed". Guess what. He did! As a matter of fact, the guy fired several more rounds as we quickly returned to the old mine on our hands and knees and dove into the shaft headfirst. What we hadn't planned for was an escape route. We were trapped. Fortunately for us, the man with the gun stayed on his back porch in the light so he was not able to see us. I guess he thought we were trying to distract him while someone else turned over his outhouses, and he was not about to abandon his post. An hour or so later we gave up and left, leaving his outhouses upright.

Once, we used the trunk of a fallen tree, some old rusty bedsprings and cinder blocks to prevent cars from passing on the only road through town. While a driver was clearing a path through the debris pile, one of us would loosen the valve core to slowly release air from one of the car's tires. We twisted the core just enough so the escaping air did not make too much noise. Also, there was always one other big surprise in store for the unsuspecting driver. As he wrapped his arms around the tree trunk in a hugging fashion to lift it from the hard top in order to clear a lane, it would feel wet and a little sticky to the touch. Since it was dark, the wetness felt like water, but it was not. We had punctured a can of black tar used with rolls of roofing paper and poured the contents on that part of the roadblock that was to be moved. Nasty!

Apparently, several years prior to my teen years, a roadblock was used in the small town of Maben, a couple of miles farther up the hollow. Maben is where we had to go fetch our mail. There was a large lumber mill located near Maben until the 1940s. The only road toward the south and west was blocked on Halloween. Later that night a car came by running too fast and crashed into the roadblock. The driver lost control and the car ran over a small embankment and rolled over landing upside down in the lake that was used to float logs from the train to the mill. Someone drowned. We never heard the whole story because nobody talked about it. The adults in our round table discussions at Herb's were opposed to our plans to block the road. It seemed that when the discussions ended up on that subject, one of the adults quickly changed the topic to something else. To this day, I'm not sure what happened nor have I ever heard who was responsible.

One other prank involved a guy about our age who also lived in town. Nobody was particularly fond of that guy, nor did we like to include him in our games because he was hard to get along with. He was always on the opposite side of every rule for every game that we wanted to play. In retrospect, I suppose he never joined our "gang". One evening, just after dusk, we bushwhacked him and tied his arms behind his back. One of our larger and stronger "gang members" helped to carry him up the hill beyond the old schoolhouse to the graveyard. We tied him to the largest headstone and left. During the night, he apparently managed to untie his hands and feet because he was home the next morning. After that incident, we all seemed to get along as he actually was a nice guy.

As teens, we spent a lot of time roaming the strip mine roads going from one swimming hole to another in a jalopy, of sorts, that burned gas that we had taken (stolen) from mining equipment. What was left of the original car that made up our jalopy was the floor, an engine, a steering wheel, the drive train, and four bald tires. The driver sat on a Hercules wooden powder box. Each passenger had to be careful of the tires, drive shaft, and hot engine and fan while cruising the rough strip mine trails. Hanging on was a chore since the roads were very rough and curvy, and the jalopy had little or no brakes, only gears. Each time before we began, we filled up with gas and oil and put brake fluid in the brake cylinder reservoir. If there was no brake fluid available we had a workable substitute - moonshine. As the brake pedal was pushed a few times, the brake fluid escaped through the worn out master and wheel cylinders. After the fluid was gone, braking was done with the gears and a mechanical emergency brake that worked as long as the driver was strong enough to pull and hold it, since the locking mechanism was long gone with the rest of the dash board.

During the couple of summers that we kept this vehicle running, we never changed the oil or water in the radiator. During the winter months, the radiator was drained, and the jalopy was abandoned, hidden away on an inactive strip mine until the following spring. By the grace of God and some dumb luck, no one suffered any serious physical injury.

When I was about 14 or so, I learned to drive on that jalopy, since we all took a turn driving it. When I was 16 my dad was injured in the mines. I received my driver's license for a dollar without taking a test because the state trooper knew that I had been driving for some time. His wife was dad's nurse during his stay in the hospital (see chapter on mine mishap) and thanks to her, I received my license. Who said we used a mule for Drivers Ed?

We drove along those strip mine roads that were called "benches"[5], because of how they were formed in the mountainside. Sometimes we drove for several miles in our old jalopy from one strip mine water hole to another. Some of those roads were almost eroded away. We always passed the mining operations' maintenance and supply areas. Occasionally, we "borrowed" a stick of TNT and an electrical firing cap or two. For some reason, the supply shacks were always left unlocked during the day shift hours.

One of the unique things that swimming in a strip mine pond presented was the three sides of high wall surrounding a bright turquoise colored waterhole that was several feet deep. Because of those depths, the water had thermal layers that you didn't experience in Slab Fork Creek. We would climb up a high wall on the mountainside, about 15 to 20 feet high, and jump into the deep part of the pond. The top layer of water was thin and very warm. The next layer was cool for a few feet, and then there was another warm layer. The last layer before the black, cold, mud was real cold relative to the hot summer air as well as the warm top layer of water.

Those pools formed when a mining operation extracted the coal seam, following the mountain contour, until the coal seam either ran out or dipped into the mountain. At that point, a huge hole was dug with the large earth moving equipment to claim every last lump of coal possible. Later those depressions filled up with runoff from rain and snow and formed the pools.

Two boys, whom we didn't know, drowned in a similar strip mine pool. From that time on, our parents forbade us from going near the pools. At that time, I was 17, and it was my last summer at home. By then the adventurous spirit fueling our desire to roam strip mines had been replaced by other things. Evidently those two unlucky boys were climbing up the loose walls of a mountainside above a pool and caused a landslide. They were swept into the water and immediately covered up with dirt while trapped under water. We had ridden a loose mountain slide into the pools many times before, luckily without injury, but no more.

Dare and double-dare challenges were alive and well among us teenage mountain boys. Our egos led us to play some games that, by today's standards, seem foolish, but we apparently were skilled and "mountain" savvy enough to pull them off without a hitch. One such

---

[5] A bench is a road dug out along the contour of a mountain. From this road "bench" earth moving equipment can expose the coal seams which can then be extracted.

game of "chicken" involved jumping off a railroad bridge into the creek as a steam engine approached.

The railroad was constructed to negotiate the narrow, V-shaped hollows that were lacking level ground.   One of the most critical problems was the grade of the railroad bed. The slope of the rails was very important because a couple of the world's largest steam engines would soon pull a hundred or more railroad cars loaded with up to 110 tons of coal out of those mountains along a serpentine route toward the seaport at Norfolk, VA. The continuity of grade was resolved by placing the railroad bed on a bench cut along the same contour of the mountain just above the flood plain.   The creek meandered in an extremely winding, curving fashion. The rail curves had their limits-of-curvature which forced the need for many pairs of tunnels and bridges. Many pairs were constructed in order to maintain an alignment that the huge locomotives could safely negotiate.

Less than a mile downstream from our little town was a bridge adjacent to a tunnel. We called that place "Tunnel Point". It was located down the Pierpoint mountain ridgeline from the main county road. Just after the bridge, two spur lines switched off the main line. The signal lamps for the rail switches were powered by burning a chemical called calcium carbide. When mixed with a specific quantity of water it produces a gas called acetylene. Acetylene burns in air with a hot, bright flame and will produce a violent explosion if put under pressure. The calcium carbide has an appearance similar to weathered limestone rocks. The railroad section crew hid large quantities of the "carbide rocks" in a crevice somewhere near the switches. We all grew up with carbide lamps that were made of brass and were small enough to hook on a miner's leather cap. The lamps held small kernels of carbide. When you metered a quantity of water from the small water tank on top of the lamp, opened the gas valve, and, with the palm of your hand, quickly came across the wheel that strikes the flint located inside a dish type reflector, the result was a loud bang as the acetylene ignited. I've done that until a blister formed inside my palm.

The carbide found near the railroad was in chunks too large for the small lamps. Carbide rocks are so hard that we could not break them into smaller pebbles. However, we did fill a Mason quart jar with wet sand; placed those large carbide rocks inside; twisted the cap tightly; and, placed the jar under a boulder in the creek and waited. Soon there was a muffled explosion followed by the appearance of a few fish floating belly up.

There was another "toy" that we made using the carbide. We used a baking powder can that had an aluminum lid that could be popped or snapped on or off. We made a small hole, with a hammer and nail, in the bottom of the can. We placed a piece of carbide rock inside the can, spit on the carbide a couple of times, and then snapped on the lid. We placed the can on the ground with the top pointed out of harm's way. Someone would hold it with his foot. Next, we struck a match and placed the flame next to the nail hole where the acetylene was escaping. With the explosion, the lid became a flying saucer as it sailed a hundred feet or so, depending on how long one waited before lighting the match and the direction of the wind.

The railroad bridge below Tunnel Point was about twenty feet or less above the water's surface. That place was our swimming hole number two. It was carved out by the creek making a 90° turn just before it passed under the bridge. The mouth of the tunnel was about a hundred or less yards from the bridge and was almost camouflaged by vegetation growing from the cut into the mouth. I visited the bridge in 2002 and was amazed at how narrow it was due to being overgrown. That is to say those huge locomotives were much wider. The adrenaline "rush" began when you were standing in the middle of the bridge waiting on a train that you could hear and feel coming up the hollow. That particular dare was to not jump into the creek until you could see the cowcatcher on the front of the steam engine.

The first time I performed that stunt, I did not realize that as the locomotive exited the tunnel, it was discharging a maximum amount of smoke as its furnace burned coal as fast as the fireman could shovel it in to generate enough steam for the hungry beast. Those huge engines needed lots of steam in order to pull those loaded coal cars up that grade. Our game plan did not include the fact that smoke had no place to go inside the tunnel so it had to exit in front of the engine. That effect provided short-term camouflage for that monster. With the track and bridge vibrating, the engine was quickly upon us. Impulsively, we jumped with just a few feet to spare. I have never had such an adrenaline rush since. As I hit the water, my legs and arms stung from the impact as my feet quickly hit the bottom hard. We were all intact with no broken bones, so our dare was a success. Maybe that is where the term "loco" originated?

Of course, when we retold the story at Herb's store you could bet that the locomotive was almost across the bridge by the time that we hit the water. In retrospect, I'm not so sure that it wasn't. What I remember most vividly are the vibrations followed by the hot water showering down upon us. The hot water was condensation from what was steam a few seconds before as the malleys (a name given to the driving wheels) transferred the energy to the rails. Those steam engines were so gigantic that when they moved using full steam power, everything vibrated including the water surface in the creek.

One hot summer day, someone issued a dare that we should go swimming in the water tower, our version of an indoor pool. What we called the "high line" railroad, was one of the spurs that left the main line at Tunnel Point. By the time it passed Pierpoint, it was positioned several feet higher on the mountain contour than the main line. That spur climbed its way toward mining operations called Glen Rogers and Glen Morrison. In southern West Virginia, within a circle of 50 miles, there are many towns whose names begin with "Glen". For instance the ones that I can recall are: Glen Rogers, Glen Daniel, Glen White, Glen Fork, Glen Echo, Glenco, etc. "Glen" is a Scottish Gaelic term for a small, secluded valley.

Two or three locomotives pulled empty coal cars, commonly called gondolas, up the steep grade and returned with a train loaded with coal. Mining operations had sidetracks so they could park empties for use between train visits.

A couple of miles up the "highline" from Tunnel Point and across from Pierpoint was a large water tower that was used to fill a locomotive's tender in preparation for the climb. *We knew about how long the engines were because we sometimes greased the tracks with heavy grease that we took from the rail switches.* That meant in order to move the locomotive and empty cars, the engineer needed to apply a lot of sand to the driving wheels. Whenever a steam locomotive starts from a standstill, the engineer spins the wheels to gain momentum. Over time the sand and the spinning of the locomotive wheels acted like sandpaper. That abrasive action wore the rail thin over time. They needed replacement every couple of years or so.

When a train had to stop on the main line for any length of time to alter its schedule before it left, one to three "torpedoes" that consisted of about a quarter pound of TNT were held in place on top of the rail with a strip of lead. When another train approached that spot the "torpedoes" exploded when the train ran over them. That was their way of signaling. Needless to say, we collected all the torpedoes that we could find. Sometimes we lined up 10 or 15 torpedoes on the rail before one of the passenger trains came by. As the train passed over the torpedoes, it sounded like a machine gun.

We climbed up the water tower to a trap door which was part of the tank's roof. After sliding the door to reveal the opening, we climbed inside one at a time. A metal ladder extended into the tank's interior. As I recall, the water level was about two-thirds full. That dare was to leave the ladder and swim to the other side of the tank and back then climb out of the tank. There was only room for one person at a time inside the small hole and on the ladder inside the tank. As I swam away from the ladder, it was not too bad a deal until, on my way back, it occurred to me that it was very dark. Besides someone's head was blocking some of the light as they made sure that I was doing what the dare called for. I made the mistake of looking up. I never saw such a small-looking hole! I remember feeling that the sooner I got out the better. I had never experienced that claustrophobic fear before as I swam toward the ladder. It certainly was a different "rush" than jumping from the bridge.

On the way down from the tower, we climbed onto the cantilevered boom that swung out over a tender to deliver the water. As we climbed toward the outside edge of the boom, someone pulled the chain that regulates the flow of water from the tank. There was another surprise as a deluge of water came rushing out onto the track bed. By the time we had figured out how to shut off the valve, that section of track had been almost washed out. I was never on the tower again.

Baptism in the Old Swimming Hole

By the time I entered high school, I was about "churched out". During any given week of the year, our family attended church twice on Sunday, sometimes on Saturday night, and prayer meeting on Wednesdays. One or two revivals held each year were added to the aforementioned schedule. Revivals were supposed to revive the spiritual awareness of the believers in the community. Revivals also meant that out of town folk brought daughters to the services. That fact eased the pain of going to church every night for a week and sometimes two weeks.

In the summers, we had church "reunions" or "homecomings" that consisted of all-day preaching with dinner-on-the-grounds. Those get-togethers probably evolved into what are now called "family reunions". All the ladies brought their special dishes of chicken, vegetables, desserts and breads. The food was laid out on several tables built with rough, uncured lumber from the local sawmill. Similar tables still dot most churchyards in those parts. I always loved the meals at those church meetings. In those days, once the young boys ate dinner, they sneaked off, missing the afternoon sessions. We knew our parents would not leave church to look for us. In retrospect, I suppose they expected us to sneak off as that "boy" behavior was accepted. Some adults thought that religion was wasted on teenaged boys anyway.

In addition to the church sessions, we had to attend a week of "singing school", and, of course, there was Bible school. A gentleman by the name of Jimmy Harold taught us how to read music notes and what tempo or beat meant to a song. To this day, I know the notes, but I cannot carry a tune. The rhythm portion of my brain apparently did not develop. However, what I did take from this musical exposure in my early life is an appreciation of what has become one of my favorite kinds of music - the old time gospel tunes, particularly if sung in a bluegrass style.

I recall a time in early March when spring had not yet pried loose winter's cold grip, and, typical for that season, the air was heavy with moisture which brought a chill that cut to the bone. Some warmth was generated from a constant shiver that didn't generate enough body heat to offset the winter chill. The water temperature was still holding onto its winter-like conditions. Only a few days before, there had been a crust of ice cantilevering from the banks about two or so inches in the slack water area between ripples where the swimming hole was located. The ice gave the appearance of an outline of white lime along the water's edge. Most preachers were generally older, so they dreaded the times when "God called them to enter those frigid waters". Spring was the time to break cabin fever, and a revival meeting was a reason to get out of the house. A revival produced an incentive for "backsliders" to confess their sins and was the best time to talk people into joining a church. In order for new converts to affirm their commitment to a church, they had to be "born again". Therefore, baptism was required.

It seemed like a lot of local people waited until early spring to join the church or to get "reaffirmed". Maybe the long, cold, dark mountain winter months gave them time to reflect upon their afterlife. My guess is that it was a case of "out-of-sight, out-of-mind". A good many folk attended church because their neighbors invited or reminded them of their spiritual obligations. In the wintertime, neighbors talking across the fence, clotheslines or from their porches was rare because of the weather.

Being somewhat southern Baptist[6] meant that when a person was baptized, he or she had to have their bodies totally submerged. Since the church that most folk attended in Pierpoint did not have a baptismal tub inside, the most logical place for a baptismal ceremony was our "old swimming hole" which was about two hundred yards from the church. That water "hole" was the neighborhood's most popular swimming place. Swimming season for us traditionally began on the first of March each year regardless of the weather. As part of a dare, it was an honor to be the first swimmer of the season. After everyone made the plunge, we were certainly well aware of how chilly the water was and how cold our bodies became before we made it home for dry clothes.

On the way to the baptism, the congregation filed from the church, singing songs as they walked slowly toward the swimming hole. It seemed as if they synchronized a song's ending upon their arrival.

The swimming hole was created by a small dam built by the railroad maintenance crew who stacked loose rocks from the creek in a mound perpendicular to the creek and about three or so feet high. Each spring after high waters, the railroad crew rebuilt or repaired the "creek-rock-pile dam" so that their water pump had enough water depth to draw water from the creek and pump it to that large water tank. Close to the center of the creek bed, there was a step-off that had resulted from erosion of some of the layers of soft shale that made up the stream floor. Shale is a rock formation that is common in coal-bearing mountains and valleys. That particular step-off was about 2- or 3-feet high. Its exact position was

---

[6] *By this juncture in this church's history, this congregation had split a few times because of doctrinal differences among its past membership, so current doctrine was probably a reasonable facsimile of the original church.*

a well kept secret by the teenage boys. Sometimes a false location was insinuated as a trick for some unsuspecting person to step off into deeper water. Most of the preachers performing the baptisms were from out of town, so they were not immune to our trick. We teenage boys were not backward when it came to springing our surprise because we knew that spring baptisms meant frigid waters. Anyone standing waist deep in frigid waters for any length of time became numb. In order to submerge someone meant that you were nearly going under yourself. The only reason that we attended the baptisms was the desire to see a preacher with a convert step off the ledge into deeper water. Of course, when necessary we came to their rescue before hypothermia set in, and we became the town's heroes!

The most desirous time to be baptized was in the summer around the end of July because of the warm temperatures before the creek became contaminated by the stagnation of "dog days". One had to avoid getting sick from the polluted waters. The risk for waterborne ailments increased during dog days. One such disease was typhoid fever which was devastating. It caused fevers, dehydration from diarrhea, and excruciating headaches and bellyaches. We all knew what typhoid did to a person from watching the reaction of affected folk who had not been vaccinated before they drank bad water. So most preachers thought winter baptisms were the lesser of the two risks. Shots were normally given in school and since most of the older folk quit school before their sixteenth birthdays to either work in the lumber mill or coal mines or become housewives, they had never been immunized. The preachers were willing to take the risk of getting sick from the cold water exposure. However, whenever possible some of the visiting preachers left it up to the local preacher to do the baptizing. There was always an urgency to baptize new converts, especially the men. Most worked in the coal mines, and death was always a possibility. No one wanted to take the risk of dying as a sinner without having been spiritually reborn.

One of the things that young boys learned early from ice skating in late winter was that the frequent warm spells caused the ice to begin to thaw and create what we called "rubber" ice. The chances of falling through were increased. We knew from experience that when you fell through the ice wearing wool long johns you didn't get as cold as you did with cotton long johns. So when we fell through the ice in the "frog pond[7]", we knew that the long underwear would keep us fairly warm while we climbed out of the icy waters and walked over the huge boulders to a hot fire. Maybe we had just invented the prototype of the "wet suit". We

---

[7] A small pond of about one-acre and less than five feet deep located across the tracks from the swimming hole. The pond was created during the railroad construction 50 years earlier. It was against the north face of the mountain so in the winter months, the sun never touched its surface.

always kept a large fire burning using old railroad crossties that the section crew discarded at that place during their summer railroad maintenance activities. Whenever we were wet, we stood near the fire and slowly rotated our bodies to absorb the heat. Sometimes when the temperature was near zero, by the time we arrived at the fire, the legs to our long johns were frozen stiff.

Since the word got out around town, probably from talk around the pot-bellied stove in Herb's store, about the warmth wool long johns provided on cold water baptismal days, preachers generally wore their newest pair of mail order wool long johns when performing baptisms. Their dress also included wool socks and a wool sweater.

One particular baptism that I remember started at about noon, as the crowd made the hymn-singing trek from the Pierpoint Church to the "baptismal hole", a.k.a. swimming hole. Everyone was milling about on the creek bank, trying to avoid the mud while jockeying for a clear view of the proceedings as well as trying to keep warm. As the event unfolded, everyone was very friendly and in a glorious mood, making sure all were aware that they were a witness to the event. Events such as a baptism caused a crowd of people to naturally huddle closer together. Cold weather had the same affect. During the milling about, most folk were trying to keep dry and keep their feet warm and safe from the mud. The mud was left the last time the creek rose in response to a winter snowmelt. The quartet of Charles "Junior" Halsey, Jr., his uncle Oak who was everybody's barber, and Junior's brother-in-law, Jesse Tolliver, and, Oak's daughter Aldene, led the singing after some church people handed out a few songbooks. Some people strained to see a songbook, but most knew the songs by heart. The quartet would then lead the crowd in another rendition of "*As we gather at the river the beautiful, the beautiful river*". During that solemn time, everyone was very quiet and respectful while contemplating deep thoughts about their individual relationship with God.

On that particular occasion, as the preacher stood about a step from the water, where the mud turned into sand, I remember him telling one of the church officials who was assisting him, to make sure that all the new converts were ready because he didn't want to dally in the water any longer than absolutely necessary. One result of our upbringing was that we had a great respect for religious folk, but we did think they were nuts for going into this frigid water. The preacher knew that before he led the people out one by one to be submerged, he had to first wade into the water to make sure that he could find a spot where the water was about waist deep. Since that preacher had been there before, he had some idea as to the configuration of the creek bottom. He also knew that the winter floods and the break up of the winter ice cover could alter the creek bottom from what it was in past years. He knew that all of those conditions could add a surprise step-off which would be extremely dangerous since most of the older women-folk could not swim.

As the crowd, led by Aldene's beautiful soprano voice, began to sing the last verse, the Reverend Sparks, squinting through his thick eyeglasses, started slowly into the cold, clear water. His experience taught him that the first time into the frigid water was the worst, so he got on with the baptism as he did everything else whenever he made up his mind. In the meantime, one of the church elders had all the new souls ready for their turn at being cleansed by their submergence in the cold water of Old Slab. They were in a neat line just above the sticky mud but close enough not to delay and prolong exposure required of an old country preacher to the harsh elements.

Brother Sparks took a new convert by her cold, trembling hand and both took short steps, feeling for the creek bottom, as they slowly waded into the cold water toward the chosen spot. We knew that the couple was perilously close to the "step-off". That old preacher was motivated to enter those frigid waters because of his faith that God would deliver upon his promise of everlasting life after death. Many of the converts went into those frigid waters because of peer pressure from husband or wife, brother or sister, rather than the promise of everlasting life. Each one also believed that they must be baptized sometime before death and that was as good a time as any. While the Reverend stood facing the convert, he folded her hands and placed them upon her breast. He placed his left hand in the small of her back, raised his right hand toward Heaven, and repeated, *"O Lord here is one of your children about to be committed to Thy service in the name of the Father, the Son, and the Holy Ghost, Amen!"* Then he laid his hand upon her head and as the convert pinched her nose, he slowly sank her backward into the water being very careful to completely submerge her body. Most of the female converts arose from being submerged in the cold water, gasping for breath while reacting with the customary emotion of shouting and saying praises to the Lord. Some men came out of the water in a more reserved fashion. After all, that was the way they were expected to react in that culture! Sometimes a person who was normally very quite and reserved would have a very emotional response to the proceedings. That outpouring of feelings totally surprised the preacher, particularly if he knew their demeanor before hand.

Any emotional outbreaks were taken as a sign that God was pleased and the convert really did receive the Holy Ghost. The Reverend led each new Christian back to shore while someone wrapped him or her in quilts and joined hands. Men took men and women took the women to dry and recover from the emotional moment of spiritual bliss mixed with ice water. Methodically, the preacher took each new convert through an identical ritual that had been performed for ages. Everyone reacted differently when arising from the baptismal cleansing as each was spiritually reborn. Each, in his own way, showed emotions as if a large yolk of burden had been lifted from his shoulders.

Finally, as the Reverend led the last person to the riverbank, he was helped out of the water, and a quilt was draped about his shoulders. He was led to the closest home for a change of dry clothes, to soak his feet in warm water, and to sip some non-alcoholic brew that had been made for that occasion. Some of the older women, my Grandmother Minerva Cook included, said that the brew contained several mountain plants that we "boys" had collected. Granny often sent me into the woods and among the rock cliffs to find certain plants for her brews and mixtures for poultices. Granny mixed and cooked the potion of wild plants according to a recipe that some say came to Wyoming County via my Great-great-great-grandfather Henry Drury Halsey, who had gotten the recipe from "Devil" Anse Hatfield's family around 1807 during a trip Drury made as a circuit preacher. The potions seemed to work well for our afflictions.

I'm sure that some of the older preachers came to the conclusion early in their careers that they would only baptize in warm water. Taking a "dip" in the March waters of "Ole Slab", particularly if you add the danger posed by taking the infamous step-off, would change anybody's mind. Most of the older guys decided to let the younger preachers handle it, since once you were infected with pneumonia, your heavenly payoff would probably come a lot sooner than later.

Serpentine Holiness

A group of folk from another town built a small, wooden church near where we forded the creek to get over to our house from the main part of Pierpoint. The church building was constructed from lumber taken from the destruction of several old houses. It was a simple makeshift structure, built with no plans, resting on cinder blocks with no footers. The floor was made from rough cut lumber, just "green" boards lain upon wooded trusses without nails. Since the building was not heated, services were not held in the cold months to the delight of the town folk. This uninvited congregation was a group of religious fundamentalists known in these parts as "Holy Rollers". We respected their right to worship as they saw fit but would rather they exercise it somewhere else. In retrospect, I don't believe anyone associated with the church owned the property upon which it was built. I suppose they built it on the creek bank assuming it belonged to no one. To my knowledge, no one protested. Mountaineers are respectful that way when it comes to anyone practicing religion.

Sometimes they broadcast their services over a loud speaker to the dismay of the whole town. That was my first experience with black and white folk worshiping together. They played and sung gospel music very loudly, which, during the course of a service, motivated a dance, called "shouting". Those who "shouted" also spoke in "tongues" after they had danced or shouted themselves into a frenzy. Whatever they were saying when speaking in tongues was a mystery to all of us and probably to them also. It sounded like gibberish to me, but I guess it meant something to them to be able to perform such a feat. It appeared to me by the time they starting shouting and speaking that they were not aware of their surroundings or what they were doing at the time.

At that point in the proceedings, the copperhead snakes were collected from their cages and handled by some. After some of them shouted and spoke in tongues for a while, they took the copperheads from the cages and gingerly handled them for a very short time before passing the snakes to another brother or sister. Apparently this was an exercise in faith and trust in God's protection and one's beliefs. Only the folk that were spiritually motivated handled the snakes on any given night.

One of my cousins, who lived in another town, was a founding member of that church. He said that one day he was walking in the woods and felt a desire to kneel down and pray. It was near a laurel patch. As he started to pray, he heard something moving in the dried leaves on the forest floor. As he parted the thick leaves with his fingers he came upon a copperhead snake that made no effort to strike him. To him that was a sign from God. His interpretation was to use the snake or its cousin to demonstrate to others faith and trust in God.

One time we boys caught a large rattlesnake and kept it in a paper barrel that was once used to ship flour. We offered the almost dead snake to the reverend for his church, but he said no, while telling us that we were the work of the devil. He was not amused! A year or two later, a flood washed the entire church away!

Pilgrimage to a County
Named for an Indian Princess

l-r: The author, his cousin, Oather Cook
and his brother, Richard Halsey
with ole Bill
at Uncle Dewey's farm
circa 1948

**Richard Halsey, Oather Cook & David
Halsey with "catch" from trout line.
circa 1948**

Chapter 7
Pilgrimage to a County Named for an Indian Princess

"Precious Memories...How they linger, ever near me..." It was mid-May of 1947, and my entire family and a few of our Pierpoint neighbors were mingling on a small knoll just below a spot where the railroad took a slice from the mountainside to form a cut with high banks on both sides. That was the highest point along a path that continued to meander down the creek bank toward a swinging bridge that allowed us to cross Slab Fork Creek better known to us as "old Slab". Our house was one of seven located on the railroad side of the creek. That knoll was the best vantage point from which we could see the road clearly through the trees as it came off Pierpoint Mountain. Our eyes were scanning the mountain road for a first glimpse of our new car when it came into view as it rounded the last curve on Pierpoint Mountain. My father and his first cousin, Ted Morgan, had gone to Mullens, about a five-mile trip over the mountain, to fetch our very first family car. Finally, the Stylemaster came into view. The bright blue Chevrolet came with a vacuum-geared manual transmission at a cost of $1,407 from Long-Well Motors, the Chevy dealer, in Mullens.

Ted and dad grew up together and were close friends. Ted was one of my Great Aunt Lake Morgan's seven sons who had been in World War II. (They all returned unharmed.) Dad, at age 37, had never had a need to drive a car, so he never learned. Ted learned how to drive when he was in the Army. Ted quickly taught dad how to drive and maintain the car. Dad easily passed his driver's test and received his license. Having a car was great, but I hated those vacuum gears. A kid could not play at driving because the gearshift would not work unless the engine was running.

Everything had fallen into place in preparation for our first family vacation. Perceptions of the location of our kin from our home were normally described in terms like "over there", "down to" or "up to". After the war, mom's older brother, Dewey Cook, had moved his family of four boys, Buddy, Glen, Oather and Lonnie, and three girls, Josie, Shirley and Patsy, from Maple Meadow in Raleigh County to a 40-acre dirt farm in Pocahontas County. Going to Uncle Dewey's farm was always referred to as "going up to". The entire family was excited about going up to Uncle Dewey's for our vacation. The upcoming adventure was all we talked about. Finally, the day arrived, and we were off on a four-hour drive to Pocahontas County to visit Uncle Dewey and his family.

Knowing that the county was named after an Indian princess and knowing her story was very exciting to us. We knew that Pocahontas was the daughter of Powhatan, Chief of the Algonquian

Indians in the Tidewater area of Virginia and that she helped the first colonists by getting food for them from the Indians. She is said to have intervened to save the lives of individual colonists. Pocahontas County was formed in the Colony of Virginia in 1821. It is now one of the largest counties in West Virginia and among the least populated.

My world before 1947 extended only from Mullens to Lester via the Virginian Railroad passenger trains, a distance of about 15 miles or so. Before we had our car, our primary mode of transportation was the railroad or walking. I had a few clues as to what was about to unfold from my West Virginia history classes at Maben Grade School, but my world was about to expand beyond my wildest imagination. That initial trip up to Pocahontas County was quite an adventure for a 12-year-old who had never been more than 15 miles from home.

As the oldest, I got to sit in the middle of the front seat between mom and dad while my five siblings jockeyed for a seat in the back. During our first trip we took the so-called "main" routes to avoid getting lost, but, during later trips, we found a shortcut or two.

With our car trunk stuffed full, and the inside of the car full of kids and mom and dad, we were on our way early on a Saturday morning in late June of 1947. The first leg of our journey was over a gravel road, Route 54, from Maben "up to" Lester and "over to" Sophia, about 10 miles. That was where we picked up the paved road. Dad explained to us that Route 54's gravel roadbed and bridges were built by the C & O Railroad in a race with the Virginian to provide access to the coalfields. That was about 1907-08. Both railroads were building bridges, boring tunnels, and laying track, within the government assigned right-of-ways, running parallel to one another. It was a railroad-building race using mostly Italian laborers. The C & O lost the race, and the State highway people used that right-of-way with all the improvements to construct a road.

We followed that route to near Beckley where we picked up State Route 3 that took us to Hinton. As we passed the southern edge of Beckley near the vocational school complex, we found our first "poi" (point of interest), a Dairy Queen! What a treat! We had never seen one before. That stop was anticipated on most of our future trips, including the return trips home. As we progressed toward a hamlet called Shady Spring, we discovered our second "poi", a fruit and vegetable stand. It was located just before starting down what appeared to us to be the longest and straightest hill that we had ever seen. It bypassed a town called Beaver. We stopped at that fruit and vegetable stand during every trip, and dad bought the ripest bananas, since they were the cheapest. That was our very first taste of a banana.

Our next "poi" was the Beckley water supply lake near Beaver. Years later as we rummaged through mom's and dad's old photos, we found evidence of several "Kodak moments" enjoyed at the lake. On that first journey to Pocahontas County, we imagined that the Greenbrier River must be a large body of water similar to that lake. Our only clues were from Aunt Lakie's letters. Aunt Lakie was Uncle Dewey's wife. When we first saw the river, mom took out the "kodak" and snapped a photo, and we loaded up the car in anticipation of what laid ahead. I remember the "no swimming", "no fishing" and "no trash" signs located just inside a fence made of a cable stretched through holes in three-foot high fence posts.

We passed through a "wide spot in the road" called Jumping Branch. Its only identification was a small roadside sign that indicated that the "town" was "unincorporated". We came upon a huge white bull that had a hump on its neck. Later we learned that it was called a "Brahman bull" and that its ancestors were from India. It was an awesome animal. Our world was expanding faster than we could fathom or imagine.

Our next big surprise came after we had descended down a curvy and steep road off White Oak Mountain into the railroad town of Hinton. There we got our first glimpse of the New River. At that point in our young lives, we thought that everything we saw was either the biggest or tallest thing in the world. Little did we imagine nor could we have known that the New River was one of the world's oldest rivers. I learned that about half a dozen years later when I took a geology course at Marshall College. As we crossed the New and continued following State Route 3, we quickly came upon the confluence of the Greenbrier River with the New. The route from Hinton continues its snake-like trail eastward running adjacent to the Greenbrier River. Along that stretch, there were a few miles of fishing camps and homes with easy access to the river.

Finally, we crossed the river and left the Greenbrier Valley onto another historic site called Talcott, the home of the Great Bend Tunnel made famous by John Henry. Of course, we all had sung the "John Henry" song about his fatal competition in 1870 with the steam-driven pile driver. As we continued down the hill into Talcott, I remember all of us looking back toward the two railroad tunnels that disappeared into the mountain that we had just crossed. It took a trip or two and some research and deduction before we were sure which of the two tunnels was the one in which John Henry had lost his life.

By now we had made our way back into the Greenbrier Valley as we came upon another "famous" small settlement called Pence Springs. We knew about that place and were awed by being so close to the locations of both the state and federal prisons for women. The state prison was on our side of the river, and the federal was located a few miles across the way on the other side of the river. The federal prison used Alderson as its mailing address. In later years, the state prison complex was converted into a bed and breakfast inn. The federal installation is still in operation. It's the prison where Martha Stewart "visited" in 2004-5 for a few months. I'm not sure if Tokyo Rose was an inmate at the federal prison at the time we made our first journey in the summer of 1947, but we knew for sure that she was scheduled to take up residency. As our very first journey continued, all of a sudden our world had gone global!

By that time, we were about halfway as we continued our trip to Pocahontas County. Each new view of the landscape was more interesting than the one before. The drive along the Greenbrier River into Alderson was spectacular as we passed all those magnificent homes that were positioned to have a river view. We had never before viewed such beautiful sites as we wondered aloud about who could afford to live like that. I recall wondering why the Summers and Monroe Counties' boundary marker was located in the middle of the bridge that connected Alderson's small business section and federal prison with the residential part of Alderson.

We soon left Route 3 and took Route 63 toward Ronceverte. As we approached the town of Ronceverte, which is French for "Greenbrier", two huge smokestacks came into view. Continuing in our mode of fascination with world records, we just knew that those stacks had to be the tallest in the world.

As we entered Lewisburg on US 219 north, the "Seneca Trail", the sidewalks and streets were alive with uniformed cadets from the Greenbrier Military School. From my studies of state history, I knew that the Seneca Trail was once a historic route. With just a little effort, you could imagine seeing a Native American hunting party making its way along the trail, through the virgin timber, toward their favorite hunting grounds in what was to become West Virginia.

The trip north on 219 was uneventful until we entered Pocahontas County about halfway up a mountain called Droop. We crossed the summit of Droop Mountain and started down the other side toward Hillsboro. About half way down, we stopped at a roadside park. There we read a sign explaining that on that mountain a Civil War battle had taken place. We were really excited that we had come upon another historic site. Droop Mountain State Park is West Virginia's oldest state park.

As we began our descent from Droop Mountain, the view of Hillsboro and the surrounding valley was breathtaking. Of course, every West Virginia grade school student knows the story about Hillsboro's most famous native, Pearl S. Buck. It's her birthplace. Ms. Buck was awarded Nobel and Pulitzer prizes for her writings. During later trips, our stop at the rest area on Droop Mountain gave us a chance to drop a dime into large field glasses for a spectacular view of the valley and Hillsboro in the distance. At that point on our first trip, we were all excited because the journey was almost over. By that time, we had been on the road for a little more than three hours; however, no one was complaining. We were all wide-eyed and alert as we had quickly changed from tourists to excited children anticipating the visit to Uncle Dewey's.

At Hillsboro we took a narrow, winding country road toward the Greenbrier River to another settlement called Denmar, about six miles from Hillsboro. That section of the trip was uneventful other than two hairpin curves, many groundhogs sunning in the fields, and acres of farmland.

As we continued our first trip through Denmar, we went down a hill toward the C & O Railroad tracks that ran along the Greenbrier River. We came upon the largest barn that I could have imagined. It was located on the riverside of the tracks. Uncle Dewey's homestead was located across the Greenbrier River from the Denmar State Tuberculosis Sanitarium for the black folk of West Virginia. That was our next "poi". It was a huge, white, multi-level structure that quickly came into view as we rounded our last curve. It was the largest building that I had ever seen. We knew that building was the tuberculosis sanitarium and that those black trustee/prisoners worked the farm that provided meat and vegetables for the sanitarium. We were "taking it all in" as we passed by.

We knew to park our car at a site near the barn. We collected our sacks of clothes and started walking up the tracks towards Uncle Dewey's which was located on the other side of the river. The farm had the river on one side with Watoga State Park and a creek called Laurel Run on the other side. Laurel Run was full of trout and guarded by timber and diamondback rattlesnakes.

Mom had written a letter to inform them on what day to expect us. Someone was supposed to be on the lookout for us during the afternoon of that day. It was about a half-mile walk along the railroad to the boat landing area. Upon our arrival, we kids hollered, and dad whistled to get someone's attention at the farm. Announcing our arrival was never a difficult chore since they were expecting us, and our cousins were on the lookout. They were always looking for an excuse to get out of doing some of their chores. Eventually someone "poled" a boat across the river to fetch us.

The farmhouse was a simple, four-room, wooden structure that included two bedrooms upstairs. One was for females, and one was for males. As a boy, I had to learn how to sleep in a crowded bed with several older cousins' dirty feet stuck in my face, when I visited their houses. I've slept in beds with three boys sleeping at the head of a bed and two or three sleeping at the foot with their feet pointed toward the head. It was not unusual for the boys to sleep on the hay in the barn loft during the summer months. Even with the occasional prick from the dried Greenbrier vine, sleeping in the barn was a treat since we could tell dirty jokes over and over again. Just to mention the first word of a joke triggered a huge laugh.

Downstairs there was a kitchen/dining room adjacent to the master bed/living/sitting room. The master, multipurpose room contained the potbellied stove that, along with the cook stove, heated the house in the winter. The master/sitting room and stove were directly below the bedroom where the guys slept. Heat traveled upstairs through a six square inch hole cut in the floor directly above the potbellied stove. In the kitchen, there was a wooden bench/table and a storage space for pots, pans and dishes plus the large wood burning cook stove. Most of the food supplies were either in the pantry, located outside next to the rear porch, or in the cellar, which was dug out just across the backyard. A washing machine sat on the back porch. It was powered by a kick-start, 2-cycle, air-cooled Briggs and Stratton gasoline engine. Everyone had to help with the chores. A couple of the chores were to keep the gas engine running and to help the girls run clothes through the wringer. Another chore that we did was to keep the wash water hot by keeping the fire going under the tub that sat on three river rocks in the backyard. By that time in my life, I was proficient in doing all tasks related to laundry.

Another source of hot water was a large water tank called a water jacket that was attached to the large wood burning cook stove in the kitchen. Above the cooking surface of the stove were two compartments called closets. These closets were used to keep food warm and to warm bread dough so the yeast would grow. On that particular stove, the warming closets had a definitive dent as a result of the explosion of a large pressure cooker during some past canning season.

My Aunt Lakie made the best yeast rolls that I ever tasted as well as the best buckwheat pancakes! The buckwheat was raised on the farm. Buckwheat flour and sugar were fed to her yeast starters that were many years old. I remember an incident that occurred when she was preoccupied with something else outside the house and forgot about her yeast rolls that were growing in the stove's closets. Needless to say, she was taken aback when she walked into her kitchen and was greeted by the yeast-fed dough attacking her huge cook stove. The entire cook top of the stove was covered.

There was a pool that was about a mile or so long in the Greenbrier River that bordered the farm. My brother Richard and I could swim like fish. That summer we instituted a tradition that every time we visited the farm our very first challenge was to swim across the river to the other side, touch the bank, and swim back. In addition to swimming, we fished and explored the surrounding property.

> *"Precious father, loving mother,*
> *Fly across the lonely years;*
> *And old home scenes of my childhood*
> *In fond memory appear."*

The things we saw and experiences we had on that first of many trips to Uncle Dewey's in Pocahontas County are some of the best memories I have. My life was changed completely when I realized that there was so much to see and learn outside my 15-mile wide world that existed prior to that trip in 1947.

On a later visit, we teenage boys got to know some of the trustees at the TB sanitarium personally. They taught us how to shoot pool, make moonshine, and, on occasion my brother and I were allowed to play softball with their team. When the prisoners traveled to a nearby logging camp, a place called Mill Creek located at the base of Kinnison Mountain, also worked by black trustees, to play ball they traveled in the back of a truck that was totally enclosed with fence wire. My brother Richard, our cousin Oather Jean and I rode in the back with those guys. They treated us as part of the team, and, when Richard or I made a play or got a hit, the other team complained in a friendly way using conversational slang that was unfamiliar to the three of us. We never felt threatened and found everyone very friendly throughout the few years that I visited before going off to college.

During the half dozen years that I had remaining before going off to college, we visited the farm several times during any given year. During one or two of our winter visits, we got to try this feat when the temperature was 10 below zero! The fun came when the clothes were hung on a line outside to dry. Needless to say they quickly froze and eventually had to be brought inside to thaw. We're been there before!

Our visits corresponded to planting or harvesting crops, butchering hogs and/or just plain visiting. We worked hard and played just as hard. One of the chores that I did not particularly like to do was required during mid-winter. That was the job of digging into a "potato hole". The ground was frozen as hard as a rock and not having a pair of gloves made it extremely difficult to dig. Most subsistence farmers stored their excess potatoes in a hole dug deep enough so the spuds were below the frost line. The bottom of the hole was scooped out so it was larger than the opening. The hole needed to be bone dry throughout the time the potatoes were buried. Several bushels of freshly dug potatoes were placed on an old blanket, tarp covered with straw. The hole was sealed with boards and tarpaper or a canvas tarp. Then four or more feet of dirt covered the boards to insure insulation below the frost line from a hard winter freeze. The potatoes lasted throughout the winter months or until needed. That storage method was better than the dark and damp environment in a cellar which was the reason that, over time, potatoes stored in a cellar sprouted and, in a very short time, were rendered inedible as well as implantable. Potatoes buried underground showed a little dryness but cooked up just as tasty as if recently harvested.

Our spring visits would normally be in March, timed to coincide with trout-fishing season. The headwaters of Laurel Run, the creek on the eastern boundary of the farm, were a stocked trout stream. At that time, trout season traditionally began on a Saturday at 6 a.m. We would leave the farm at three or so in the morning and hike several miles toward the headwaters to find the best fishing holes. Several visiting fishermen chose to enter the stream at the headwaters, which extended into the populated portion of Watoga State Park. We spent many hours along Laurel Run throughout the spring and summer. The creek provided a way to cool off, and the water was clean to drink.

During the dryness of fall or Indian Summer, we had our first of many encounters with the native Timber Rattlesnakes. In the summer months the trout congregated in deep, cooler waterholes. It was not unusual to be standing knee deep in the cold water while fishing in one of those small "blue" holes. There was always a pile of debris consisting of old trees and limbs at the end of those holes. We made it a point not to travel along that bank. Frequently, we spotted a rattler sunning on one of those debris logs. If it stayed put, we just kept on fishing and left it alone. The rattlers were loners and wanted nothing to do with humans, so as we fished they slowly crawled into the brush.

Springtime was when dad and Uncle Dewey visited the stock market in Marlinton to purchase several young piglets to fatten up over the summer and fall. Dad had developed a reputation for always purchasing a runt or two because they cost less and fattening them presented a certain challenge.

During the springtime, we also helped plow the fields with a team of horses and a "260 Lynchburg" turning plow, and we helped sow the field crops, mostly corn, beans and potatoes. After we "turned over" the garden with a fork-like spade, Aunt Lakie and the girls planted and cared for the garden. The garden was located adjacent to the house so wild animals could be kept out. Vegetables, such as onions, tomatoes, lettuce, cucumbers, peppers, mustard greens, kale, and sweet potatoes were grown in the garden. The anticipation of when each could be harvested was almost as rewarding as eating the vegetables. I visited the onion patch many times and ate many young green onions with a piece of cornbread while sitting against the fence where no one could see me.

Uncle Dewey had purchased a team of very young and untrained horses from his older brother Fred. He transported them from Maple Meadow which was near where we lived. Their names were "Bill" and "Minnie". Being somewhat young, the team had a lot to learn which made them unpredictable in some situations. One of my earliest experiences in handling a team of horses was plowing with Bill and Minnie. Since my cousin, Oather Gene, and I were still not fully-grown, it took both of us to handle the horses in a working situation. One of us handled the reins and the other tried to control the direction of the plow so the furrows were straight. The Lynchburg plow cut a deep furrow, and, at the end of the "run", the blade had to be flipped or turned to the other side of the plow in order to fill in or turn over the ground into the last furrow cut while going in the opposite direction. That plow was so heavy that, as we turned the horses around, we had to make sure we used their power to flip the plow's blade so we could go in the opposite direction.

One day Oather Gene was handling the horses' rein, and I was struggling with the huge plow in an attempt to plow a straight furrow. Neither one of us wanted to be plowing. We would rather have gone fishing in the Greenbrier River. However, we knew that this section had to be plowed first. I'm not sure exactly what happened to spark the altercation, but somewhere along the way the plow handles moved as we were turning around and knocked me over. I landed on top of Oather. Once the plow started over, there was nothing I could do to control the situation until one of the handles rested upon the ground. Needless to say we were not happy campers as we began wrestling, rolling and tumbling in the newly plowed field. While the horses were enjoying a brief rest, Oather's big brother, Glen, arrived to cool us down. He took over the plowing. Glen was always the mediator as he had a demeanor of even temperament that always brought a calming force to any situation. He always had our unquestionable respect. He had the patience of Job as he taught us skills such as how to use a crosscut saw, how to plow, how to skin raccoons, groundhogs, and squirrels, how to survive in the wild, and many more mountain survival techniques.

We tried to ride the horses after a day's work was done, but they were so wide that our legs didn't go down far enough to hold on to their bare backs. I remember the muffled echoes coming from the ground as the horses ran or trotted across the barnyard. It was a hollow sound like crossing a bridge covered with dirt. Years later, after I took a geology course at Marshall, I realized that we were in limestone country and that there may have been a cavern or an undiscovered cave below the barnyard. We never knew.

During the long rainless days of summer, we worked 13-hour days, particularly when hay had to be cut, dried and stored in a stack or in the barn loft. The hay was cut with a mowing machine that was pulled by the team.

Transporting hay to the barn was accomplished by taking a 15 to 20 foot sapling and tying a rope to the large end. That end was then attached to the horse's harness with a rod called a single tree. The small end of the pole was away from the horse. The small end was pushed on the ground under the center of the hay pile. The piles were about the size of a Volkswagen Beetle car. Then the rope was wrapped halfway around the top of a hay pile, looped around the small end of the pole, then brought back toward the horse by wrapping it around the opposite half of the pile and then tied off at the big end of the pole. Horses are not very bright, but you could turn either horse loose anywhere on the farm, and each one would start to walk toward the barn. As the horse made its way to the barn by itself, we would nonchalantly meander in that direction, putting off the time when we had to help pitch the hay up to the barn loft. In every instance, we had to lead the horse away from the barn and back to the field.

Eventually, we got around to building a haystack. They were built around a 10- or 15-feet pole erected in a well-drained, desirable feeding location in the field. After the barn loft was full, the excess hay was placed in a stack. A pole was sunk into the ground, and the hay was stacked around the pole to about 10 feet or so.

The thing about "haying" that I didn't like was not the long hours but the fact that there were three neighboring farms where we had to harvest their hay also. That came about because in subsistence farming each neighbor owned different pieces of equipment that was necessary to cut, rake, turn, and transport everybody's hay.

One of the more dangerous chores that I learned to perform at the farm was harvesting oats with a scythe called a cradle. A cradle was constructed by attaching a frame of wooden fingers, which was about the same length and parallel to the scythe blade for the purpose of catching the cut grain. Each swathe of the cradle generated an armful of cut oat stock. Our cradle was set to be swung in a circular motion from the right side with the left hand catching the cut oats. On the follow through, the left hand gently laid the cut oats on the ground as the right hand positioned the cradle for the next swathe. After the grain was dried on the ground for a day or so, several bundles were gathered up and tied into a shock. The shocks were stored in a stack. If you were not very careful and not concentrating on the chore at hand, you could cut a huge gash in your leg with the scythe blade. Being somewhat coordinated, I came through each time in good order, at least in better shape than Uncle Dewey did.

One day Uncle Dewey picked up the dried oat bundles to tie into shocks for stacking for winter feed. As he placed his hand under one, he jerked it back commenting that it must have been a yellow jacket that stung the back of his hand. Yellow jackets are very bad during harvest time, and they live in holes dug in the soil. Uncle Dewey, figuring that the yellow jacket could not sting him a second time since they lose their stinger and life as a result of one sting, stuck his hand under the bundle again with the same result. That made him mad, so he stuck his boot under the bundle of cut oats and kicked it over. There to his amazement was a small copperhead snake protecting his cool home. After making an effort to suck the venom from the four fang marks, his hand was swollen for a few days, but healed OK.

True Value

One time my cousin, Oather, was continuing the breaking in process for the young team of horses, Bill and Minnie. That time he hitched them to a large wooden wagon with wooden wheels covered with metal rims called tires. That wagon was just like the ones you see in western movies, but we had no canvas covering. During a slow drive through some small trees in the shallow woods of Watoga State Park, something spooked the horses, and they started to run into the deep forest. They were running freely with my cousin in the wagon and holding the reins but not in control of the horses. As the team was galloping through the timber, one horse went to the left and the other to the right of a 4- or 5-inch diameter tree. Evidently the wagon's tongue, made of hickory wood, hit the tree point blank and shattered breaking some of the leather harness straps and the chain link that connected the wagon tongue to the horse collars. Neither animal was hurt in this stunt, evidently because the harnesses provided some protection for their bodies by distributing the forces of impact throughout the network of leather harnesses. Everything that was broken could be fixed on the farm except the broken chain link. The broken chain link required the services of a blacksmith, which cost money that was not readily available.

Later in the week when my dad arrived at the farm from his workweek in the mines, he took Uncle Dewey, the boys, and the broken chain to a blacksmith who lived on a farm located just as you start up Droop Mountain going south on US 219 out of Hillsboro. For about 3 or 4 hours the farmer/blacksmith labored over an anvil, taking time to turn the hand crank which operated the air blower that kept his open air furnace hot. He would heat, pound, shape, measure and quench a piece of metal as it took on the shape of the broken chain link.

After the blacksmith had finished making an exact copy of the link, Uncle Dewey asked him, "How much do I owe you?" "Would 25 cents be fair?" the blacksmith asked. That was my first lesson in "true value".

Coon Huntin'

One night while we were hunting raccoons, which was legal from 6 pm to 6 am, we went up one of the many small creeks that empties into the Greenbrier River. The particular branch that we selected to travel along up the mountain was spring fed with a small stream flowing through rock filled potholes creating small pools with plenty of nettle weed growing along both banks. As we made our way upstream, I remember wishing for a clear area soon because I was tired of climbing through the wet brush and being stung by the nettle weed that you could not see in the dark until it was too late. We only had one light, and the batteries were being saved until we treed a "coon". In any case, the light was adequate to see well enough to shoot the coon out of a tree. Uncle Dewey had two hunting dogs. The younger one was a Blue Tick Hound, and the more experienced one was a Black and Tan. The young dog had to be on a leash until we were ready to hunt because he was a free spirit. He didn't take direction very well. I suppose he felt that anything that moved was fair game. That guy would run off from the hunt and keep going. Whenever that young dog left, we could always find him sleeping outside the kitchen door at the Denmar Sanitarium. The cooks had taken a liken' to him, and, when he showed up at their door, they gave him a hunk of beef. He was a smart dog.

Once we turned the dogs loose to hunt coons, they knew what to do. They just followed their noses. The older dog knew the smell of raccoons and, for the most part, ignored deer, wild cats and other critters. The younger dog was another matter, but he was learning. Since that was my first "coon hunt", I remember most of what happened that night. Seeing both dogs disappear in the dark, I thought the hunt was over. But that was not to be as both dogs reappeared, moving back and forth excitedly. Their noses were close to the ground, which contained rocks and nettle weed, while running at about three-quarter speed. Finally, the older dog broke out with a bass-sounding bark. He had picked up a fresh scent. The pace quickened as the scent became stronger. Both dogs disappeared into the dark, and their bark produced a muffled echo from the hillsides. That sound meant that they were still trailing the critter. Once they had the raccoon up a tree, they barked skyward, producing an echo. Also, when the dogs spotted the critter, their barking frequency really revved up.

I soon received my first lesson in the laws of physics. When a force, the dogs, was greater than the movable object, me, and then the resultant was that I was going to be displaced! Once the dog's bark indicated that the raccoon had been treed, we picked up our pace to quickly arrive at the site. Trekking through the woods at night over wet, moss-covered boulders the size of a kitchen table with nettle weed pricking your bare hands was not what I called a fun Saturday night, but it was exciting. That was one adventure that I would not have missed for anything. After we arrived at the site, the dogs were collected and leashed. For some reason, I got the job of holding the dog leashes. With someone holding the spotlight, my older cousin, Glen got a bead on the raccoon and shot him with a single shot 22 rifle, but the coon didn't fall from the tree. We decided that the critter was dead but was hung up on a fork in the tree and would not fall to the ground. Cousin Glen decided that the prudent thing to do was to climb the tree and dislodge the coon. In the meantime, I was standing on a damp moss-covered rock, slightly up the hill from the tree, holding the dogs' leashes. I was not prepared for what happened next. As Glen climbed the tree poking the coon's carcass with the empty rifle barrel, he finally dislodged it. In doing so, he had positioned himself too far out on a limb, and it broke about the same time the falling coon hit the ground.

Needless to say, I could not hold the dogs back any longer as they began pulling me down hill on the slick rock and through the nettle weeds. I distinctly remember as Glen fell through the tree limbs, he was screaming for me to hold the dogs because he did not trust their judgment as to what to attack. I had no choice but to let go of the dogs, since together they were bigger than I was. The dogs took about two jumps down the hill to cover the distance as they attacked the dead critter. As it turned out, those dogs really were man's best friend since Glen was bruised but unscathed by the dogs. As a matter of fact, I believe they were trying to protect him.

I remember one snowy night on a coon hunt a few miles up Laurel Run when we came upon an old camping trailer. It was obvious that the trailer hadn't been used in years, but we were cold and tired and needed some heat to warm up our bodies. The trailer had what appeared to be a workable stove inside. Once we got the fire started, and it began to feel cozy inside the trailer, I stood upright in a corner behind the stove and, while leaning against the wall I dozed off. As the stove and flu pipe began to get hot, they began to crumble. Pieces were falling to the floor. On top of the trailer where the flu pipe came through the roof, there were several years' collection of pine needles, which promptly caught on fire. Inside the trailer, we found an enamel pot that held about a half gallon of water and ran outside toward the creek, a few feet away, to fetch water to douse the fire. The creek was frozen solid, and as we tried to break the ice with the pot each time we hit the ice, some of the enamel overlay popped off. Eventually, we collected enough water to put out the fire and left.

Thanksgiving-Hog Killin' Time

As soon as school closed for the Thanksgiving holiday, my brother Richard and I caught a ride with a cousin and arrived at Uncle Dewey's the weekend before Thanksgiving. Mom, dad and sisters, Edna, Margaret and Helen along with my baby brother, Sidney, came up sometime during mid-week. Since that was the time spent killing and processing hogs, Uncle Dewey and his clan needed our help.

Preparation for hog butchering began in the fall with the gathering of firewood. Fallen trees of about 6 inches or less in diameter were dragged, using the team of horses, to a site near the hog pen where the hogs were processed after killing. The woodpile was created after an adequate supply had been gathered and stacked near the house for use during the winter months. All of the firewood was sawed with a crosscut saw to a certain length and split into several triangular shaped pieces that would fit into the kitchen cook stove as well as the potbelly stove.

Once split, that length of wood was ideal with which to build a fire around a 55-gallon metal drum. The drum was laid on its side and tilted about 45 degrees with the closed end buried about half the length of the drum. The open end was supported with flat rocks. In that position, the drum was capable of holding enough water to completely cover a hog's body. Also, there was enough drum exposed to allow room to build a fire that was kept burning around the drum's sides to maintain the water temperature at near boiling. Once a hog was submerged in the boiling water for a few seconds, its hair could easily be scrapped from its body with a butcher or hunting knife. A hoist was built directly over the open end of the drum, with three small logs, so the hog could be lowered into the drum and then pulled out and left hanging to facilitate butchering.

During the 1940-50s, there was still an adequate supply of chestnut wood lying on the forest floors. The chestnut tree had been wiped out of the Appalachian forest several years earlier because of a blight disease. Over the years, the wood had seasoned while lying on the forest floor and, as a result, was easy to split which in turn made excellent kindling wood. It was said that moonshiners preferred to burn chestnut wood to fire their distilleries because the wood did not produce a detectable smoke plume. Wormy chestnut wood is still in great demand by furniture makers.

Thanksgiving was the ideal time to butcher hogs. With no refrigeration on the farm, the cold weather allowed time to prepare the pork for storage. Plus, all the "laborers" were on vacation from the mines and/or school. During that special season, each day began a few hours before daylight as the fire had to be built to heat the drum of water to a boil. Hot water had to be available before the first hog was shot. We stored water in several old wooden rain barrels to use in replenishing the water lost after each hog was doused in the drum. Once the killing began, the fire had to be maintained to keep the water in the drum boiling.

After a couple of guys carefully herded a hog as close to the hoist as possible - hogs would not get too close to a fire - someone calmed it down for a few seconds while it was shot in the head. Care had to be taken with the hog because they are mean and not afraid. Also, care was required when shooting the rifle with people all around. We all knew about gun safety. We used a single shot 22 rifle with "short shells" to initially stun a hog's brain. I learned the correct way to shoot a hog, and, since I was perceived as being a calm person, I became the shooter. The correct spot to hit on a hog's forehead was at the intersection of a 45-degree imaginary line from each eye. If hit at that exact spot, a hog would fall in place. The shooter had to level the rifle even with the hog's head. Bullet impact instantly rendered the hog unconscious, and it quickly slumped to the ground. Immediately, someone, generally Uncle Dewey, severed the jugular vein, and the unconscious hog bled to death producing the "other" white meat. As soon as the blood stopped flowing, a loop was cut using the achilles of each hind leg. A "single tree" was attached with a metal hook into the tendon, and the hog was hoisted up, doused into the boiling water being very careful to get the hair hot and loose but not start cooking the meat. Once that was accomplished, the carcass was hauled from the drum and lowered onto a makeshift table of boards lying on the ground. Each one of us took a knife, found a spot and start scraping off the hair. After a few days of pouring hot water over a hog, thereby steaming our hands that were exposed to the cold air while scraping hair, our hands would chap to the point that it felt like most of the outer layer of skin was missing.

Once all the hair was removed, the hog was washed off and again hoisted up to begin the serious butchering processes. Once hanging, the hog was gutted, and all the organs were removed and saved in wash pans. Normally, our main dish or our traditional dinner (lunch on the farm) was baked liver from the first hog butchered.

Once the hams, shoulders, "sow belly" or "fat back" (bacon), tenderloin, lard, and other pertinent parts were separated from the carcass, they were carried about a quarter mile to the smokehouse and kitchen for processing. The women started the process of rendering the lard and hand grinding parts of the shoulders to produce sausage. The sausage was mixed with the appropriate seasonings and hand rolled into balls and placed in quart glass Mason jars. Several of those open top jars of sausage balls were placed inside a large pressure cooker and cooked for a time. Later the jars were removed with sterilized tongs, and the lids were retrieved from the cooker and placed on the jars. As the jars cooled, the lids sealed. The sausage could be stored in the cellar for many months.

The hams, bellies and shoulders were sugar cured and hung in the pantry next to the kitchen, high enough so that mice could not collect a free meal and, in the process, ruin a ham. Later the bacon was sliced from the lean portion of the hog's belly and smoked in the smokehouse, which was located on top of the cellar. The smoking process was one chore that I hated as much as the job of stuffing hay in the barn loft, or worse still, scraping the hair off a dead hog. We repeated that process for three or four days until we had butchered eight to ten hogs.

After my very first experience with "hog killing", I remember that there was a large chart hanging on the wall at the Otsego Company store's butcher with drawings on how to cut up a hog. The poster displayed a dissected hog showing all the traditional "cuts", naming each one. During the next year, I made an effort to spend some time with the company store butcher and learn all I could about butchering hogs. I remember him being very helpful as he took the time to teach me how to handle a knife to create certain cuts of meat. By the very next Thanksgiving, I had proven to Uncle Dewey and dad that I knew how to make the proper meat cuts and how to prepare the carcass for storage. After the first hog was killed, I was allowed to accompany the carcass

David Halsey

back to the pantry and help process the dead porker. From then on, there was no more scalding water, shooting hogs, or scraping hair for me!

"Ronceverte"

After the farm chores were done on any given day, we grabbed a bar of homemade soap, which was made from lye and strong enough to take the hide right off your back, and headed for the river. Whether we fished before taking a bath followed by a swim to wash off the soap, depended upon how hot it was.

Since most of the time, more than one family of cousins visited the farm at the same time, there was always someone who did not know how to swim. We, generally me, gave them a safety lecture about the hazards of getting in over one's head in the river and drowning. The adults always expected me to be in charge which was OK by me. On two separate occasions, while my brother and I were swimming in the middle of the river away from the opposite bank where the non-swimmers were, someone stepped into deep water. On both occasions, our cousins had waded into the water, about chest deep, and they could not resist taking one more step. In both cases, they were in over their heads and were bobbing up and down like a cork, gasping for air all the while getting into deeper water. There is an old wife's tale that we all had heard most of our lives, which states that "after you go under the third time, you are gone". Well after those two occasions, I could bear witness that the tale was not true. In both instances, I quickly swam over to the guys in trouble, being very careful that they didn't grab me and drown us both. As I approached, I dove to the bottom of the river and grabbed them by their ankles and slowly pushed them shoreward until I was sure they could stand up with their heads above the water's surface. One of our "dares" that subsequently helped in a rescue was one that challenged us to hold our breath underwater. My best time was about a minute and a half. Of course, without a watch and counting 1000 and one, 1000 and two, etc., we did not have the most precise timing device.

Within a week of each of those incidents we taught both cousins how to swim in water over their heads. With 20-20 hindsight, we should have made that a requirement before being permitted to enter the river. We never told our parents about either episode. However, for many years afterwards when we visited at family or high school reunions, those cousins always asked if I remembered when I had rescued them and thanked me. What a feeling!

Poison Ivy

It was late one summer day. The adults had no demand for our time as the chores were done, and swimming, fishing and gigging frogs were on the schedule. Before we could get going toward the river, someone heard a yell coming from the railroad on the other side of the river. It was our older cousin Eugene and his wife Polly. We quickly got to the boat, an old battered Army surplus pontoon boat that was powered by a long pole. That is, until we came along. We swam alongside, holding on to the boat as we pulled it across the river to the landing site. They loaded their camping gear and food onto the boat and back across we went. Since there were already 20 or so folk at the farmhouse, Eugene and Polly came prepared to camp. Besides they probably wanted their privacy, but they tolerated us. We helped them set up their campsite. By the time they found a level spot along the riverbank, it was beginning to get dark. While they erected their tent, we collected firewood and started a fire since they needed to cook supper. In the past, rattlesnakes had been seen near that location, but we knew the snakes were loners and avoided people, if possible. We never thought twice about the dangers of running around barefooted in old worn out trousers that had the legs cut off to create our swimming trunks. We had already eaten supper so after they ate, we decided to spend the night at their campsite, which was OK with them. I remember in the dark near the fire, making a bed outside the tent from the leaves and shrubs that I could fluff up, and we boys slept like logs as I always did.

The next morning I woke up realizing that, while trying to sleep on the hard ground, I had turned and tossed as I lay in a patch of poison ivy. I didn't recall ever having gotten infected by poison ivy, so I thought no more about it as we began to enjoy the day with our cousins. Wrong! Taking a bath in the river with homemade soap was not on our schedule since that day was not a Saturday. In fact, in the summer we swam nearly every day, so we did not need a bath, at least we thought so.

A couple of nights later as I was trying to find a comfortable spot in the hay in the barn loft, I began to itch. The itch started on my arms and legs and then progressed to the rest of my body by morning. I spent the night scratching all over without any relief. The next day a rash appeared on my skin and my private parts began to swell. By then I knew that I was in some kind of trouble, so I informed my dad of my predicament. He immediately took me over to see one of the black doctors at the Sanitarium. He examined me and told my dad what medicines that I needed but that he legally could not prescribe medicine for me unless I was a patient at the facility. However, he said that if dad got the medicine that he would inject the prescribed doses. So we visited a doctor in Hillsboro who wrote the prescriptions. After being injected daily for about a week, I was cured. Needless to say, I have avoided poison ivy ever since!

In spite of all the perils presented by the local critters and the hard work necessary to survive on a dirt farm, my journeys to the land of Pocahontas were the best!

The Versatility of Slab Fork Creek

Pierpoint, West Virginia

circa 1960's

House on the right is where

David grew up

with Slab Fork Creek behind the house.

circa 1953

Chapter 8
The Versatility of Slab Fork Creek

"During these years, David's mother was bedridden with a serious illness. Since David was the oldest of six children, he was responsible for many of the chores. They lived so far from everything-school, a town, etc. that they never went back out in the evenings for school functions or any other activities because transportation was a problem."

"Every Sunday he had to carry three to four tubs of water from the creek to do the family's laundry. He had to do this on the weekend because during the week the water was filled with coal dust from the mines. When he got home from school on Mondays, he did the laundry in a big wash tub. In the springtime he got out of school to help the Department of Natural resources to stock trout streams. During crop season he had to use a hoe to work the field to get it ready to plant. He helped canning foods, and he helped make "chow-chow" and apple butter" - Jason David Halsey 1989

My dad hired several women who looked after my five siblings and me, and they did housework whenever my mother was having a bad time. By that time in our young lives the frequency of mom's health problems was increasing. Six free-spirited youngsters were a handful for a healthy person to look after much less an ailing one. I remember one lady in particular who came to live with us to do the cooking, washing, ironing, and other household chores. She was very good to us, and we all seemed to get along until my brother and I began to tease her. Her name was Margaret Lester. She stayed with us for several weeks, and she liked to talk. During our conversations with her we discovered that she had been married a few times, and we found out what all of her married names had been. As a matter of fact, we referred to her by including all her married names - Margaret Lester Higginbottom Belcher White Ford! My brother and I gave her a hard time by doing things that we should not have done or not doing what we were told to do. We got into trouble. We made sure that our name-calling occurred before dad came home from the coal mine. She always promised not to tell on us if we would just shut our mouths. We would, and she did not report us to dad. Bless her heart!

I remember when Slab Fork Creek, our only source of wash water, was teeming with aquatic life. Smallmouth bass that grabbed a hook baited with a hellgrammite, grasshopper or minnow and ran with your line until you decided to set the hook in its mouth. Bass were plentiful in every pool formed above every ripple throughout the creek's length.

We spent hours with a treble hook, taken from an old fishing lure or plug, dragging the three hooks across the nest trying to snag a bluegill that was protecting its eggs. The bluegills patrolled the perimeter of their oval-shaped nest in a random fashion being alert to the need to confront any intruder. We also spent countless hours trying to snag a bottom feeder called a "hog sucker". They were about a foot long and would lie quietly on a rock in the deep clear pools. They were not very tasty.

Further up the food chain were the muskrats. They were numerous and very active. We trapped them, harvested their pelts and shipped them to a company in Minnesota. Toward the bottom of the food chain was another creature that we called a "water dog". That guy was a huge salamander, 8 to 10 inches long including its knifelike tail, with short legs and a head that resembled a catfish. As a matter of fact, the thing resembled a species of catfish called a mud cat with legs. Also, there were several varieties of turtles, snakes, and other critters present to round out the creek community.

Shortly after the Second World War, aquatic life in Old Slab was essentially destroyed by the clouds of coal dust fines that flowed downstream as discharge from the washing operations taking place at the Maben mine tipple. There were no water quality regulations[8] at that juncture.

One area not affected by the black water was located across the tracks from our swimming hole. It was a mysterious pond, positioned at the base of the hill below the highline tracks on the north side, that was created when the railroad was built. One of the mountain runs was cut off, and the flow from the stream created that pond over a 60-year period. We used to take a long hair from a horse's mane, float it upon the water surface, and, over time, we believed it magically turned into a long slender, swimming, snake-like creature. As I matured, I began to realize that the gentle mountain breezes moving effortlessly across the pond's surface caused the hair to appear to "wiggle" on the water. As the air cooled on the mountain slopes, it slowly began falling down as the evening cooling cycle began. Since the hair did not have enough mass to break the surface tension of the pond, it appeared to float magically as mosquitoes or water bugs have done for eons. Unbeknownst to me at the time, as I journeyed into scientific maturity that phenomenon would eventually be explained to me.

Maben began its existence as an upstream sawmill town. After the War, it quickly matured into a coal mining camp as the public need for harvesting one natural resource, timber, gave way to another, coal. The late 1940s and early 1950s were the beginning of the era of cleaning coal to be competitive in world markets. Old Slab was an ideal source of water. It provided an adequate supply, was easy to pump to the tipple and was convenient to discharge back into the stream. Years later the pure coal fines left in the settling pond were commercially mined. As a result of those coal-washing operations during the week, the creek at our house was clear, being void of coal dust fines that made blackish soup, from late Saturday evening until mid-Monday morning. So come Sunday, whether

---

[8] *Today the stream has recovered its aquatic quality and quantity.*

there was rain, shine, sleet, snow or hail, enough water had to be toted using two peck pales up the bank to fill four number three washtubs.

There is an old wives' tale that says "Appalachian women were tough because they could have a baby on Monday and still get out the wash that same day"! In that neck of the woods, having Mondays as washday made sense. As a matter of fact, it seemed to be a logical choice when one considered the other activities that had to be coordinated with washday. Dad's dirty work clothes, after spending a week inside a coal mine, were always brought home on Saturdays. The temperature inside the mines remained near a constant 54 degrees. In summer or winter, dad always layered his mining clothes. From the outside in, he wore a denim jacket, coveralls, flannel shirt, cotton pants, long underwear, and several pairs of socks. Sometimes in the winter he wore another outer coat.

Another reason for doing the washing on Mondays was the availability of the washtubs. Those were the very same tubs that we used for our Saturday bathing sessions, so they had to be empty by Sunday.

Water from the well had too much iron mixed with sulfur which made it unsuitable for doing laundry. Our only source of wash water was from Slab Fork Creek. So much for being Baptist and resting on the Sabbath! My brother and I tried to get out of carrying the water to no avail, so after a time we just did it without protest.

If the steep creek bank behind the wash house was not wet and slick initially, then it was after several trips of sloshing water from the buckets. We knew that the faster we carried the water, the sooner we'd be finished. For some reason, my memories of doing the wash only include the winter episodes. Great care, particularly in the winter months, was taken not to fall down since the result was a loss of two buckets of water, muddy clothes, and a wet, cold body until the chore was done. Sometimes to relieve the boredom of carrying water, my brother and I would have a "windmill" contest. That required taking a full bucket of water and swinging it in a circular motion, 365 degrees, over our heads without spilling a drop. As I grew older and stronger, I could "windmill" both buckets together without spilling a drop. It's a wonder that arthritis has not visited my shoulders' rotator cups because of those pranks.

One of the number three tubs was positioned about a foot above the ground on three flat stones so that after school on Monday a fire could be built and maintained to heat the water in the tub. After the water was brought to a boil, there was always a "scum" on the water surface that needed to be gently lifted off. The tub and fire were located just outside the wash house door on whichever side that shielded the fire from the winter wind. Also, the fire was located far enough away from the wash house so it was not a hazard, even though at times we thought about burning it down, particularly in subzero temperatures. The remaining two tubs were placed inside the wash house so the ice, which would form over night, did not become too thick. Generally, during the winter months, a fire was built in an old potbellied stove inside the washhouse. The fire was started late on Sunday and banked to smolder until morning when the grates were shook, and the fire was banked[9] again before we left for school. That small amount of heat helped cut the winter chill inside that uninsulated wash house. As a matter of fact, the wash house offered very little protection from the outside elements during the winter. Winter washdays were always cold in Appalachia.

After my brother Richard and I came home from high school on Mondays, it was already dark as we built the fire under the tub. Sometimes when the cold winds were whistling down through the hollow, we had to shield the tub with a sheet of tin roofing. Otherwise, the water would never boil. After the outside fire was burning hot, we took care of the fire inside the wash house. The grates were shook to "wake up" the smoldering fire that had been "banked" with coal that morning. While everything was slowly warming up, we ate supper, changed into "old" clothes, which means non-school clothes, collected the dirty clothes from the rest of the family, and separated them into the appropriate piles to get ready to wash them.

I can still remember the feeling of the winter coldness on my wet and chapped hands as I put the wet heavy clothes through the old washing machine wringer. Our wash house was built using "rough-green" lumber from the local sawmill. It was the same kind of lumber we used in our outhouse. As the vertical boards "cured" or dried out over time, each board shrank leaving a crack between almost all of the remaining boards. During a snowy, winter Monday night, the wind found every crack through which to blow snow inside the wash house. Even with the potbellied stove going full blast, that is to say the flue pipe took on a glowing bright red halfway to the ceiling, snow accumulated on the floor where it was the coldest. Since the fire emitted only infrared rays, it only heated up that with which it came in contact. As a result, the stove, for that matter any heat source that burns fossil fuels, only warms the side of your body that's facing the fire. That means if it's real cold, the other half of your body freezes[10]. During the winter nights when the temperature dropped below zero, to stay warm we had to slowly turn, like a rotisserie, to collect enough heat over our bodies to stay reasonably warm as we tended the washing. I recall on several occasions having clothes that had just been taken from the rinse water and run through the washer wringer freeze in the basket while waiting to be hung on the outside clothesline. Try hanging those clothes in the dark in subzero weather!

---

[9] *Banking a fire means that coal is put on the flame and the airflow through the damper is cut to a minimum thus the fire burns very slowly and can last for a couple days.*
[10] *Years later I flew an army aircraft that had a cockpit heater which dumped hot air just above the right foot which at a frigid altitude would warm half of your body the very same way, which is why I probably thought this was normal?*

One of my favorite and most rewarding things to do on washday was to search the pockets in dad's dirty mining clothes looking for chewing tobacco. Because of the ever present methane gas that could cause an explosion, miners were only allowed to chew tobacco underground rather than lighting matches for cigarettes. Dad's favorite chewing tobacco was called Beechnut. It became our favorite chew at an early age! Normally in a good week, we found three or four nearly empty pouches in the pockets of his work clothes. Sometimes we mixed the chewing tobacco with fresh bubblegum, which produced a chew that lasted all day. In fact, when we played American Legion baseball, a chew of tobacco mixed with bubblegum lasted through a doubleheader!

After we washed the clothes with a soap powder called Rinso, they were dumped into a lye solution followed by a rinse in clear water. The whites, which we classified as anything from grey to white, were rinsed in a tub of water laced with bluing. By that time, our chapped hands were blue. That was followed by hanging the clothes on an outside clothesline located in the yard next to the house. In the wintertime, it was not a fun job to hang clothes outside since they quickly froze, as they swung in the winter wind, like a board. Beginning on Tuesdays, the clothes, piece by piece depending upon what we wore for the rest of the week, were gathered and brought inside the house to thaw and to continue the drying process. Sometimes we ironed the flannel shirts and denim overalls to aid the drying process.

Our washer was an old worn out electric Maytag. When you tried to pass the heavy denim through the wringer, you had to hold the wringer mechanism with one hand and guide the clothes with the other hand. Regardless of how much soap powder was dumped into the hot water along with the lye, there were never soapsuds visible in the washer because the water was so hard with minerals. Whenever the overalls were put through the wringer, the pockets were full of wash water, and, as the wringer clamped down on the pants passing through, that water squirted into our faces. That necessitated an immediate eye rinse with cold water since the lye and soap mixture burned both eyes as well as taking the hide off your jaws. Somehow we all survived quite nicely, healthy and wiser!

Truth Is Stranger Than Fiction?

Folk there believe that "things" happen in threes. The three stories that I'm about to describe all happened one October more than 60 years ago. Each occurred along Slab Fork Creek.

In the spring my bachelor cousin, I'll call him Clarence, had settled back in at his mother's house after serving in WWII. He had ordered a bunch of baby chickens from the sponsor of a country music show that aired on WCKY radio station in Cincinnati. In a few days' time, they arrived intact via Railway Express. During that summer he provided lots of TLC, and the chickens thrived. Clarence had built a coop just out back of his mother's house so he could oversee the chickens' well being.

Late one night in October, Clarence was awakened by a disturbance in his chicken coop. In the mountains in October, it can be very cold after the sun goes down, so most men start wearing their long john underwear around that time of year. Since a trek down the path to the outhouse on a cold night must be quick, there was no time to fool with a lot of buttons. Generally, the back flap was left dangling from one button which provided quick accessibility. That night was no different. Clarence slowly got up and grabbed his double-barreled shotgun that he kept loaded with no. 10 buckshot ready to protect his flock. As he quietly approached the chicken coop, he used the end of the gun barrels to raise the latch and began slowly opening the door. Meanwhile, there was a large black and tan hound dog sleeping on the back porch next door. He recognized Clarence and decided to help him out. Once the hound crept up to Clarence's backside, he did what all dogs do. He began to sniff Clarence to make sure that he was who the dog thought he was. As luck would have it, the hound stuck his wet, cold nose inside the back flap of Clarence's long johns. At that instant, Clarence had the coop door open about halfway. He reflexively pulled both triggers discharging both barrels. All of his chickens were killed instantly! Clarence was devastated!

Later that week, the second "thing" that happened was this. My father and a neighbor had planned to kill a heifer that my father had purchased in the spring from a man who needed the money. We were experienced hog-butchering folk, but that was to be our first experience at butchering a cow. Since he worked six days a week in the Otsego coal mines, my dad decided that Sunday was the only day that he could butcher the heifer. From the start, mom was against killing that cow on a Sunday. She further warned dad that the "devil would show his ugly head", but, my dad figured that he had no choice.

Early on a Sunday morning the heifer was tied with a piece of clothesline wire to a large West Virginia mahogany tree. Outsiders call that tree a poplar. The game plan was that Clarence would load a "pumpkin ball" in one barrel of his shotgun, and he would shoot the heifer. The neighbor, who said that he was experienced, would cut its throat and jugular veins. All agreed.

Clarence took dead aim at the cow's head and pulled the wrong trigger of his double barrel. He shot the heifer with no. 10 buckshot, only scalping the animal and putting out one eye. The neighbor started to cut the throat as the stunned heifer regained its composure and became very irritated. The neighbor only managed to cut the hide of its throat. He missed the jugulars. Realizing the dilemma, Clarence remembered that the "pumpkin ball" was still in the shotgun, so he decided to fire it to sever the jugular. He decided for safety's sake that he would aim at the throat with the poplar tree in the line of fire. All agreed, and he aimed and pulled the trigger. The instant before the gun discharged, the heifer seemed to remember what had happened before, and it flinched. The "ball" went directly through the cow's throat, missed the jugulars and hit the tree cutting the clothesline wire.

Now there was a mad, one-eyed, scalped, and very much alive heifer on the loose running through the hamlet. In the meantime, a teenage neighbor girl, who had heard my mother warn dad about the devil, ran toward home screaming "it's the devil". She was the same girl that used to follow us boys around and tattle on us when we did something that we should not have done. That was until the time we found a six-foot black snake in the barn, turned over a no. 3 washtub, put the snake under it and placed the girl on top. She stayed there for almost two hours. She never followed us again.

Nearly all the town's people followed the crazed heifer as it approached the cut and started down the hill toward the tracks. We weren't sure if the cow would end up in "Old Slab" or on the railroad tracks. Finally, the heifer fell to the ground next to the railroad tracks. Dad and his helpers butchered it into parts large enough to be transported home in our wheelbarrow. Once the heifer "parts" were back home, it was properly butchered.

Pierpoint had not had so much excitement since Aunt Gertie got her left breast caught in the washing machine wringer. If you had ever used a gasoline washer, you would know that when you put a wet pair of heavy miner's overalls through the wringer, you must feed the overalls with one hand and hold the wringer with the other hand. Otherwise, the ringer would spin around with the rollers spread about half an inch apart as the overalls passed through. When the rollers were in that position they got mighty hungry. Besides, Aunt Gertie was a large person who had nursed 12 babies. Well, you get the picture.

The third "thing" involved domestic critters and happened later that October. It involved a hog. Dad had purchased the half-grown pig in the spring. We fed it table scraps, cracked corn, lumps of coal and some weeds that were edible. Pigs/hogs love to eat metallurgical coal because its soft, has fiber, and is full of calories.

The cracked corn mixture came in 100-pound sacks that were made of cloth with print designs. That was the reason that the ladies accompanied us to the store on days when we bought feed so they could pick out the patterns on the sacks. They eventually sewed the cloth into dresses.

In any case, over the summer and fall, the pig grew into a hog that subsequently fed our family of eight for a year! It's a tradition in those parts to butcher hogs during the Thanksgiving holidays because of the cooler temperatures that helped to overcome the lack of refrigeration. Also, the miners were on holiday. Our hog pen was out back near the creek and far enough away to cut down on the smell in July and August. One year when the creek flooded, another hog drowned while trapped in the pen, so dad moved it several feet higher on the creek bank.

Sometime before daylight on a Sunday, the hog had rooted around the rail fence until it had created an escape route. Under the cover of darkness, the hog wandered away unnoticed. I recall that we did not miss the hog until we started to "slop" (feed) the hog late Sunday evening. We searched the town, asking questions and hiking up and down the railroad tracks until dark without any sign of our hog. Dad had not ruled out the possibility that someone had stolen the hog.

What we didn't know was that a railroad section crew had just finished doing some emergency repairs on the switches near Tunnel Point. While the crew parked their equipment on one of the sidetracks awaiting the passage of a freight train, they saw the steam locomotive strike the hog and knock it over the railroad bank. Since that was Sunday, and the section crew was collecting overtime pay, they decided to take the time to bury the hog. They did so in a shallow grave.

On Sunday night everyone had to get to bed early. Dad had to get up at four in the morning, prepare breakfast, arrive at the mine bathhouse, change into his mining clothes, and be prepared to supervise the mining operations before the miners arrived. We kids had to catch the school bus. That particular night dad had to have gone to bed thinking that "there might be something to this devil thing, and maybe mom was right after all".

At about three in the morning, mom was awakened by a noise on the back steps. She arose, went to the kitchen, pulled the string to turn on the light, got the broom that was leaning on the door frame, and opened the back door expecting to find a dog trying to get comfortable on the back steps. As soon as she looked in the dim light shining outside, she screamed, threw the broom up in the air and ran back through the house hollering "it's the devil". She went out the front door into the darkness. Dad was awakened and went to the back door to investigate. There stood the lost hog with half of its face missing, covered with coal dust and cinders without an ounce of energy left.

Dad sent my brother and me into the night searching for mom while he went after Clarence and our neighbor. At the first light of day, the hog was butchered. As I recall that was the last hog that we raised at home.

Those are some of the peculiar things that happened nearly 60 years ago in a small settlement called Pierpoint situated by a creek that the natives called "Old Slab", deep within the southern Appalachian Plateaus.

Mine Mishap

Otsego Mine
circa 1951

Chapter 9
Mine Mishap

*"He said that his father is definitely the person who made a lasting impression
on his life. His father was a coalminer. His left arm was nearly cut off in coal mining
machinery when David was 16. David was in a theater where he always went on Saturdays
and stayed all day. Someone came to get David and his brother because their dad had been
hurt. That night David and a neighbor took his dad" arm-which had been amputated-home
from the hospital and put it in a box. David, by himself, buried the arm and never told
anyone where it was buried until very recently." -Jason David Halsey 1989*

The summer of 1951 was the most difficult time of my young
adult life. I did an innocent favor for a buddy. It turned out to be a dumb
move on my part, and I got into some trouble with the railroad and the law.
After spending a night in the county jail, the good judge, R.D. Bailey,
failed to document the incident so I had no "record".

As a teenager, my world continued to expand. I considered each
conflict to be a learning experience as I continued my journey into
adulthood. Generally, on Saturdays when dad had to work in the mines,
my brother and I spent the day at the movies. Mullens had two theaters.
On Saturdays they showed a cowboy movie, a serial with weekly perils
of some adventure, cartoons, newsreels and other features. We always
arrived early, around 10 AM or so, depending on our luck with
hitchhiking. We stayed until the last bus[11] left Mullens for Pierpoint at
10 PM. All we needed for a successful Saturday was a total of fifty
cents. The bus ride cost ten cents, the theater cost fifteen cents, and a
Coke and popcorn together cost fifteen cents. When we hitchhiked to
Mullens, we saved a dime. If we could successfully sneak into the
theater, we saved another fifteen cents that afforded more eats and drinks.

Mine Mishap

The last full measure of climatic summer had turned into a hectic
time for dad. It was Saturday the first of September 1951. It was a day
typical of a summer that was almost over. It was the time just before the
school year started, and the signs of fall began to appear. Plants and trees
were poised to all the majestic colors that these southern West Virginia
hills can project in autumn. Dryness had dominated the weather for several
weeks. The trees that draped the gorgeous mountains had lost their green
brilliance to a dull bluish-green, a sign of moisture deficiency. Some
Yellow Poplar and Sycamore, located in the narrow V-shaped valleys near
Slab Fork Creek, had already begun to lose their inside leaves, and poison
ivy and Virginia creeper were taking on a rusty, bright crimson glow.

My recollection as to what happened on that day is sharp, vivid in
detail yet vague in purpose. The events of that day left a clear and deeply

---

[11] Bus service from Maben to Mullens began late in the 1940's.

etched memory in a young son's thoughts, to the point that every day thereafter always contained a thought relating to that incident. I will never forget it. Some of the minute-to-minute happenings have faded into that oblivion called time, yet most of that day's events are as vivid as if they occurred just yesterday. One day scientists will learn how this knowledge is stored in our brain's memory banks so that recollection is simple, precise and vivid every time. I suspect that knowing what the surroundings were and basically what events took place allow one the luxury to fill in the blanks with perfect detail, doing so with an uncanny ability to be factually clear over time.

Morning always came early for dad. The last few weeks had been frantic, to say the least. It was Saturday, the sixth straight day that he had worked a ten-hour shift in the coal mine. That had been his schedule for as long as I could remember. He was extremely tired. Typically, he came home from work, grabbed a bite to eat, and then spent his evenings helping dig out a basement under the Pierpoint Community Church.

Coal mining was at its peak of production as well as at an all time high economically for the parent company, Oglebay and Norton. That company had owned The Brule Smokeless Coal Company at Otsego since 1936. Wages were moderate, and every employee that could manage their finances was living comfortably. Dad did that exceptionally well as he worked every day that he could from 1928 until "that" day, Saturday, September 1, 1951. Dad spent twenty-three years in that coal mine without an incident. Every cent that he earned went toward the betterment of our family's standard of living. He never withdrew a dollar in company "script". Script was a way to receive wages earned before payday. Script could only be used in the "company store".

Following World War II, recovery provided a heyday and a romantic time just before the fifties era took hold. The entire country was becoming mobile. The mystique was wearing off from nearly two decades of Democratic presidents. Bituminous coal miners had been working six and sometimes seven days a week. There were large demands for metallurgical coal that looks like sparkling black diamonds. It was so carbon pure you could ignite it with a match. It was coal that from which you could almost squeeze the oil. It burned smokeless. It contained a lot of energy per unit. That coal contained more calories per pound than any coal yet discovered anywhere else on earth. That demand meant it was not uncommon for miners to work two shifts some days, which was referred to as "doubling back".

Dad had progressed to management as a mine foreman in a progressive company that provided him with many rewards that improved the quality of life for our immediate family. By that time, the six children ranged in ages six to sixteen. Growing pains and a lack of individual challenges that could bridle a maturing and curious male child, namely me, had begun to cause dad some heartache. There were no outward signs of emotion, but now that I have grown children, I can understand what he may have experienced. He must have felt his "chaps" were perfect, and proof otherwise was difficult for him to accept. Yet he allowed room for individualism and mistakes. He made allowances for each of us to progress along the learning curve called maturity. By that time, my brother, Richard, and I knew that if any spanking took place that dad would do it the instant the misbehavior occurred or no spanking took place. Plus, he always administered discipline at home, so we knew the trick was to never arrive home at the same instant he did. Thus, a whipping was avoided. My quess is that he knew about our strategy!

At four a.m. dad ate a hard-boiled egg and biscuit and fixed a pan of Quaker rolled oatmeal so that it was ready for our breakfast when we awoke. His lunch was put into a round, metal miner's pail with a container full of milk. By a quarter to five, he was on the road driving over the three miles of narrow, winding, mountain road to the Otsego bathhouse to don his work clothes. In 1951, the bathhouse was relatively new. Previously, bathing was accomplished in our kitchen using a "number three wash tub", since we had no indoor plumbing. Prior to about 1947, dad left home dressed in his work clothes and walked the three miles to the mine, mostly along a railroad track. He made that trek for about nineteen years during which time, by shear chance, he missed being caught in two train wrecks.

That particular morning was greeted by a blanket of fog shrouded over Old Slab, faithfully meandering within and just above its banks as the calmness of the morning air allowed stability until the fog was consumed by the morning sun. A morning sun that dad had hardly ever seen for most of his adult life. Once on the mountain road, State Route 54, about three quarters from the mountain top, he could gaze over the steep bank where he could see by moonlight for several hundred yards to the creek where the fogbank appeared as a long mass of interlocking feathers meandering in and out of the brush seemingly protecting the creek banks. Once around the first few of several dozen curves, the creek disappeared into the dark abyss of night not to return to view until the end of his journey as he descended the mountain to the bathhouse. At Tunnel Point where the road reaches its highest point on the mountain, about the halfway point for him, dad later told us that a bird flew into his windshield. That was not a good omen in that neck of the woods. Dad said that he thought about turning back, but he was not too superstitious so he continued on as the thought was soon crowded from his mind as he planned the preparation activities for his shift. He must have arrived at the bathhouse totally preoccupied, deep in thought. That was a mental state that would cost him dearly about six hours later.

The bathhouse was a cinder block building, whitewashed and rectangular in shape. It was about two and half stories high. On the inside was a large open room containing about 20 showerheads, all covered with a rusty orange-colored stain. The iron-laden water contained more than enough minerals to be considered "hard water". In the outer cove were the foreman's dressing room, lockers, showers and their office. The men changed into their work clothes inside the "great room". Their "lockers" were chains anchored to the ceiling through a pulley system. One end of the chain contained a hook and small basket for belongings. The clean were put in the basket and dirty hung beneath it. Each chain could be locked to the wall or unlocked, and the basket and hooks lowered to the floor so items could be interchanged. It was rather an ingenious contraption that was efficient and provided a safe storage area for personal items.

Dad changed into his coal dust-saturated work clothes in the foreman's room. That was the sixth day for those work clothes so each piece was covered in dirt, particularly the long underwear which had long ago taken on a hew of grayish black from their original whitish gray. After donning the long johns, the overall denim pants and flannel shirt were next and the coveralls after that. The legs were taped over the boots to prevent coal dust and the constant 54-degree air, being extracted from the ventilation system, from going up the legs. The next item of clothing was the denim coat. The thick leather belt containing tools and the battery for the electric light on the miner's hard hat were put on next. Finally, the BeechNut chewing tobacco, lunch pail, note pad, time book, and mine maps were loaded. Then the half-mile walk to the mine opening was achieved.

At the mine mouth, the Link belt appeared perched upon perfectly round rollers that gave the black ribbon of the belt a smooth ride to the hum of the powerful electric motors that supplied the energy. Dad always stopped at the dispatcher's shack before entering the supply room to get a headlamp with a recharged battery as did every member of each shift. Also, he had to gather the latest information on the conditions at the mine face, plus allow the "fire boss" time to safety check the mine for methane gas. That was a chore that had to be done between each shift. Dad also had to determine if enough workers were present with the required expertise so that the shift would be successful. He accomplished all of that before entering the mine.

Soon the miners that had worked the "hoot owl" shift arrived on the outside via the belt. Once they were outside the mine mouth, the belt was reversed to transport the day shift and supplies inside. That was the only time that supplies could be taken inside the mine. Careful planning and coordination was always needed by the foreman and supply people. Those folk performed an early version of critical path scheduling, doing it manually for many years before it became popular with the aid of computers. Early on, mine foremen were required not only to determine what supplies were needed for the next shift, such as rock dust, electric wire, light fixtures, air dock explosive devices, lubricants, etc., but they were also required to determine in what direction to mine. They had to make surveys, draw mine maps, measure methane gas, determine rock dust quantities, and make timber and crib calculations. They also had to coordinate a crew of men running cutting, drilling, scooping, loading, and conveying machines so that a 28- to 34-inch high coal seam could be extracted safely and economically. Those few men who could successfully perform those tasks became mine foremen. Dad was the best according to his peers. As the section foreman, he was responsible for whatever happened on the dayshift. The day shift contained the seasoned veterans with tenure because it was the prime time to work, and veterans got first choice of shifts.

My guess is that it was then about 6:15 as the shift gathered at the mouth exchanging pleasantries. That was a ritual, as each man spoke to dad and any other foreman, calling them by their first names. Dad responded to workers calling them by their first names. That was an important ritual because doing so meant acceptance as well as that those were folk that you trusted with your life. The crew was always referred to as "men". It was a given that you had to be a "man" to work in a coal mine. That verbal greeting demonstrated respect. Dad had earned respect early on, so whatever he said was almost never questioned. He knew that and accepted the responsibility with a quiet pride and a never-ending sense of determined responsibility. He was quietly revered by those who would not accept responsibility and respected by peers who accepted whatever challenges life offered.

One after the other, as if in a rehearsed formation of acrobats, dressed in denim and covered with coal dust, each miner from the hoot owl shift peeled off the moving belt in perfect timing, being cognizant of the roof location, just like a chorus line of dancers. Immediately following the last man who was the shift foreman, the belt was stopped then reversed so men and supplies could be hauled inside for the day shift. Dad oversaw that everyone was on in a prone position with heads down. "Start 'em up!" he probably yelled. Into the mountain's bowels they rode.

Afterwards, no one was sure of the exact section in which they worked that day, but after a couple of miles of an undulating ride inside the mountain, the crew arrived at the mine face. That was typical of the routine that dad had followed since 1928. It was a trip that he would never take again. It was a ritual that ended that day.

Upon arrival at the mine face, each man went about his particular chore, as if orchestrated as part of a precision-trained team of professional fossil fuel extractors working in the most highly mechanized coal mine in the world. The crew consisted of drillers who drilled holes for the "Air Dox"[12] to explode. That was the way to safely shatter and break the coal from its natural state without fear of a gas or dust explosion since there was

---

[12] The Air Dox is a devise that uses compressed air to form an "explosion".

no fire flash involved. There were men who operated the cutting machine that sliced about 3-5 inches of coal from the bottom so that when the "shot" went off, more coal was broken from the face with less energy than was required if "shot from the solid". Men kept the area around the loading machine, called the "duck bill", clean from coal that spilled over its short conveyor belt as the "duck bill" scooped up the loose coal after the shot. Any coal that could not be scooped with the machine had to be shoveled by the men. In order to shovel coal in a vertical space of less than three feet, a miner had to lie upon his belly and use his arms to gather coal toward his front. That motion is similar to the one used to make an angel in the snow except that you are on your belly instead of your back.

There were men whose function it was to build and set the timbers and cribs[13] in the appropriate places. Men spread rock dust onto every exposed crack and cranny of the coal seam to reduce the chances of a dust explosion. Men shoveled coal to keep the machines clear. They also were responsible to keep the crew in mining supplies from the stockpiles stored inside the mine. There were men who "fire bossed[14]", and men who bossed the overall operations such as dad. He could, did and would do any job that his section crew was required to do so that the assigned number of cuts were made. The crew had to load their quota of coal to get a full day's pay and still end the shift after 8-10 hours. Each shift was assigned a certain amount of coal to extract. At that time, coal was extracted by using a technique called "room and pillar[15]". Each man knew how many "rooms" of coal had to be mined for each shift. An efficient crew could complete a shift an hour or so early.

Dad's crew was special to him, because everyone carried his own weight. There were no "gold brickers". Both "white" and "black" worked as a team inside the mine but were segregated outside the mine. That bothered dad, but he never talked much about it except to show respect for his fellow man and to provide help if needed and requested. He helped if asked, but he never pried.

That particular morning things apparently went well except that one of the men whose job it was to run a cutting machine got sick and had to be replaced. Since that machine performed a critical job for the crew, it had to be functioning. Since dad was the only other person who was available that could run the machine, he took over the job.

By lunchtime, he was exhausted, both mentally and physically. He ate his lunch evidently in a daydream. He later said that he was leaning against a timber close to an electric motor that drove the belt. The

---

[13] Timbers and cribbing were used to prevent the rock from falling. Timbers were normal ling use unless the mine roof looked dangerous, and then a crib was built for support.
[14] A Fire boss performed a safety inspection inside the mine between each shift.
[15] Coal was extracted which created a room about 20+/- feet square. On each corner of the room a pillar of coal was left to help support the roof.

vibrations provided a massage as well as warmth from the constant 54-degree environment that the mine provided year-round.

For whatever reason, there was an unprotected roller installed on top of the belt. That was probably to prevent the belt from flopping up and down due to the slack caused by the pulsating surge of the huge motor, located about two miles away at the mine mouth. The motor had to strain to generate enough inertia force to overcome the weight of the coal on the belt and to keep the belt moving at a constant speed.

After dad recovered and we had seen his pocket watch that he had stuck in the chest of his bib overalls, he and a couple of his crew related the following events of the accident. At about 12:28 PM, Saturday, September 1, 1951, dad subconsciously turned to push off from a timber as he attempted to rise onto his knees under the low ceiling. It was a maneuver he had done many times before. His gloved left hand missed the timber, which was not unusual since he was in a cramped space and was not looking, and hit the running belt. He flinched too late as the roller and belt in unison with lightening speed gobbled up his hand, his forearm, upper arm and quickly began gnawing into his rib cage. In an instant, the grinding chewed his upper arm, muscle, bones and tendons into a dangling mass of meat. Finally, the hungry monster turned him loose as the men stopped the belt and began to render first aid. Dad knew he was seriously hurt and in life-threatening trouble. He also was aware and had reasoned that he must get to the outside if he was to have any chance of survival. He threw the dangling remnants of his left arm and hand over his right shoulder and around his neck, and he told the startled crew to put him on the belt for the ride to the outside. He also told one of the crew to call for an ambulance to meet him at the mine portal and to be ready to haul him to the hospital.

The journey from the "face" to the outside must have seemed to him to take an eternity. Dad was in a state of semi-consciousness trying to deal with the possibility that he might die. His thoughts were of six fatherless "chaps" left to an unhealthy spouse who would be challenged to complete their mental and physical growth. His reality must have produced thoughts about dying at age 42, such a young age when he should have lots of life remaining. He knew he might not have the chance to enjoy grandchildren nor a chance to do more things that make life worthwhile. He had a strong willpower and was determined not to let that happen as long as there was an ounce of life left in his mangled body.

His thoughts may have included an earlier evening spent taking apart a safety lantern used to detect the presence of gas in an underground coal mine. As the "fire boss" at that time in his career, he needed to make absolutely sure beyond any reasonable doubt that the "safety lamp" was working since everyone's life depended on that small blue flame. In the old days, canaries were used to detect gas. Whenever gas was present the canary would die quickly giving people a chance to evacuate to the surface.

Dad must have had thoughts of all the past explosions that blew mangled bodies and human parts out of the mineshaft into the tipple screens, which I witnessed as a five-year old, and of all the belt fires that required carrying casualties from a dense, black, smoke-filled mine to the safety of the outside. He knew that in every mine related mishap that involved fire, explosions, slate falls, or machines almost always caused death.

As he said later, memories went through his semi-conscious mind in a flash. He had thoughts about all the hunting and fishing trips he had made to Pocahontas County, West Virginia. Also, he recalled the many nights "coon" hunting and the resultant suffering from the night air that aggravated his hay fever and sinus allergies. He wondered how he was going to squirrel hunt with a shotgun with only one arm. Briefly, a thought may have crossed his mind about how he was going to help slaughter pigs at Thanksgiving time, only a couple of months away.

Dad gave verbal outbursts of directions to the "men" who were feverishly and nervously trying to evacuate a weak and incoherent man who they revered as their boss. His fear for survival was so vividly expressed that he wanted to be taken to a larger hospital at Beckley, 30 miles away instead of the smaller hospital in Mullens, only three miles away. The "men" knew that he would not survive the Beckley trip so there was no choice.

Later dad told me that he had made no promises except to take whatever was his lot and make the best of it, nothing more-nothing less. By the time the men had transported him to the mine mouth, the ambulance was waiting.

By that time, he had drifted into a state of unconsciousness. His body was reacting to the traumatic shock of having the left limb nearly torn from the shoulder. Loss of body fluids was soon to become the critical issue for survival. Subconscious thoughts occurring now would not be realized until a few weeks later. The body's reaction, both mentally and physically, to the shock of possible termination is a mystery. A tranquil sleep is self-induced by the brain which short circuits the severe pain of severed nerves. The brain produces thoughts that cause pleasant dreams while blocking out the fact that the entire body's survival defenses are being generated so the critical organs, needed to sustain life, can survive. Thus, the body can endure. He encountered thoughts of peaceful scenes, such as angels and doves dancing on the windowsill of his hospital room, coupled with a serendipitous feeling. Oh the brain is a wonderful organ.

Amputation was followed by transfusions utilizing 16 pints of rare "O Negative" blood. The blood was donated by many volunteers who had answered the call over WWYO radio that Ralph Halsey needed help. He spent several days near death. Later, dad awoke in the Mullens General Hospital to discover that he was alive minus an arm; he had eight broken ribs with most of the skin covering gone; he had a broken collar bone; and, he had feelings never before experienced. He later recalled those feelings as he wondered about how his father had felt after losing a foot and part of a leg in the same mountain at the young age of 19.

He said he awoke with an uncontrollable craving for oyster stew. He had not eaten in six days. Helen Wolfe Halsey, his sister-in-law, married to his only brother Woodrow, lived near the hospital. She obliged, as she did many times while he recuperated, by bringing him the stew. Aunt Helen is a most gracious lady.

Dad says that he remembers waking up in the operating room, feeling a twinge and hearing something hit the floor. That something was the remnant of his limb, which I buried later that night. Before the hand and arm were buried, a ritual based on superstitious beliefs was performed. It had to be done since there was no harm in doing it and since some believed that not doing it could produce unknown results. A dear friend and trusted neighbor, Vescar Rhineheart, brought the arm from the hospital wrapped in the same white sheet and towel that the surgeon had placed the ground up mass in earlier when he severed it from dad's torso. The hand was put on a board palm down, fingers straight and both the hand and arm were taped securely to the board. That "proper" positioning was supposed to prevent the arm and fingers from hurting dad in future years. Everything was rewrapped with the same sheet that came from the hospital and put into a wooden box. I buried the arm at an undisclosed location and never told anyone where it was until after dad died in 1983. He never knew where I buried it, and he never asked. I think he thought I had buried his arm in between his mom's and dad's graves on the mountain above Pierpoint. I did not! In time, dad's wounds healed, and he lived for another 32 years, dying of natural causes in his 74th year.

If there can be a day when one makes the transition from child to adult, then that was the day for me. Late on that Saturday, September 1, 1951, I became a man because I was the oldest and had to take on the family's responsibilities.

Dad's nurse at the Mullens Hospital was the wife of a West Virginia State Policeman. One day while dad was still recuperating in the hospital she asked my mom how we were traveling to and from Pierpoint. Mom responded that neighbors were driving us. The nurse looked at me, a 16 year old big kid, and asks if I could drive. I had been driving make shift cars on strip mine roads since I was 14, so I said yes. She asks my mom for a dollar and about a week later my driver license arrived in the mail.

Epilogue

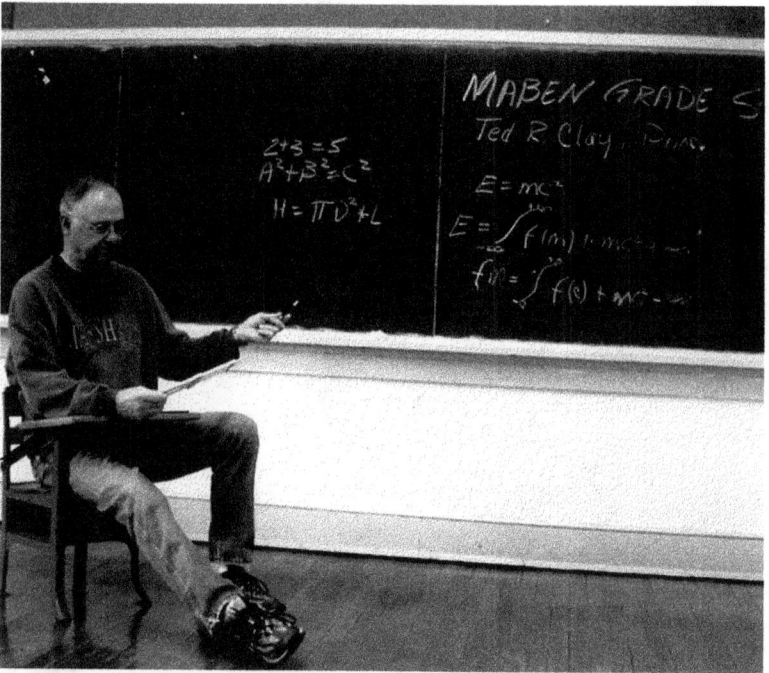

David, with the slide rule he used
to earn an engineering degree
from Marshall University,
sitting in a chair from Maben Grade School.
His love of physics is represented on the board.
Neither Maben Grade School nor
Mullens High School no longer exist.

Epilogue

"The path from cradle to grave is filled with so many perils it's a wonder that we reach the latter." Unknown

"Up another Notch"-*David attended Marshall University in Huntington, West Virginia on an academic scholarship. His major was engineering, and he minored in physics and military science. He said his grades were "up and down." He was one of ten to graduate out of one hundred and one who started engineering when he did."*

"In his free time he got together with his friends and just like college Students do today, he drank beer and chased girls. He lived in various apartments off campus."

While attending the University, he worked at a funeral home that had an ambulance service. David drove the ambulance. He also drove a hearse. He greeted people at the door when they were visiting a deceased. He helped with the embalming. After this job, he worked at a barbecue joint where he "hopped the curb" and worked the cash register. He then worked on a survey crew. He found his jobs very interesting because he was so eager for new experiences."

"During his military he became eligible in six branches of the Army: Artillery, Aviation, Armor, Corps of Engineers, General Staff and Civil Affairs. He flew for the Army National Guard for twelve years."

"One of the most dramatic experiences he ever had involved a military assignment as Operations Officer in charge of planning how to find missing people and to clear the debris which were the result of the disaster caused by the Buffalo Creek dam failure in southern West Virginia. There were a series of mining camps along the creek that were devastated by the failure. At the end of the assignment when the debris had been cleared up and the water level went down, three young children's bodies were found. Having three children of his own at that time, the real scope of the disaster hit David very hard." -Jason David Halsey 1989

As a teenager, my dream was to become a civil engineer and fly military aircraft. I did both by the time I reached my mid-twenties.